American & European Postcards of HARRISON FISHER ILLUSTRATOR

Reference Book
Price Guide & Collector's Checklist

American & European Postcards of HARRISON FISHER ILLUSTRATOR

by Naomi Welch

Edited by Kim Zeigler
Photographs by Tony Grant

AUTHOR'S NOTE

The author has made every effort in the preparation of this book to ensure the accuracy of the information. However the information in this book is sold without warranty, either express or implied. The current market values in this book are for postcards in very good, excellent, or in near mint condition. Postcards in mint condition will demand higher values than those listed. Postcards in good, average, or poor condition reduces the card's value based on the card's overall condition. For more information regarding postcard grades refer to the section on page 213 titled *Grading of Postcards*. The market values should be used only as a guide, and are not intended to set prices which may vary from one section of the country to another. Auction prices, as well as dealer prices, vary greatly and are affected by condition as well as demand. The author will not be held responsible for any losses that might occur as a result of consulting the price guide and collector's checklist.

Copyright © 1999 by Naomi Welch

All rights reserved. No part of this book may be reproduced or transmitted in any form or by any means, electronic or mechanical, including photocopying, recording, or by any information storage and retrieval system, without permission in writing from the author.

ISBN 0-9670212-2-7
Library of Congress Catalog Card Number: 99-93667
U.S. Place of Publication: La Selva Beach, California
Printed in Hong Kong by Dai Nippon Printing Company. For information contact:
DNP America, Inc. 50 California Street, Suite 777, San Francisco, CA 94111 (415) 788-1618
First Edition

List of full-page images:
Frontispiece: *A Spring Blossom*
Page 10: Harrison Fisher
Page 17: *I'm Ready*
Page 113: *Stringing Them*
Page 181: *Over the Teacup*
Page 185: *The First Evening in Their Own Home*
Page 191: *Looking Backward*

Additional copies of the following books may be ordered from:

Images of the Past
309 Playa Blvd, Suite 107
La Selva Beach, CA 95076-1737

The Complete Works of Harrison Fisher @ $39.95
American & European Postcards of Harrison Fisher @ $34.95

Add $4 postage for each book within the United States
CA residents add 8% sales tax

DEDICATED

To

Raymond

my husband, for his encouragement and support.

Christina and Kendall

my daughters, for their ongoing patience, and love.

Floyd and Charlotte

my father and mother.

ACKNOWLEDGMENTS

Creating a reference book required an immense amount of energy and time. I wish to express my sincere thanks to the members of my family and to my collecting friends who supported and encouraged me throughout the entire project.

To Raymond Welch, my husband, for sharing my dream in making this book become a reality.

To Christina and Kendall, my daughters, for their ongoing patience, and love.

To Charlotte Zeigler, my mother, for her untiring and endless hours of care she provided to my daughters while this book was being written. Without her, this book would not have been possible.

To Kim Zeigler, my sister and chief editor, for her judgement, advice, and beautiful way with the English language which contributed so much to this entire book.

To Joseph Lee and Emma Mashburn, for their encouragement to write this book, and for their willingness to share a wealth of information on Harrison Fisher postcards, and on the world of publishing. Joseph Lee and Emma are authors of several postcard reference and price guide books. Their accomplishments include *The Super Rare Postcards of Harrison Fisher*. This reference book provides detailed information on the history and origin of the rare Finnish cards, and is a must for all Fisher collectors.

Special thanks must go to my collecting friends, Carol Groesch and Robert Kaplan, who provided several rare postcards featured in this book. Their participation allowed readers to view postcard images not otherwise available.

Table of Contents

Acknowledgements
Introduction 11

1   AMERICAN POSTCARDS
Book Advertising 18
Product Advertising 21
Rare American Postcards 23
Detroit Publishing Company 26
Reinthal & Newman 29

2   EUROPEAN POSTCARDS
Austrian 114
Bulgarian 115
Danish 116
Finnish 122
French 154
German 155
Polish 157
Russian 158

3   OVERPRINTS & VARIATIONS 181

4   FRAMED POSTCARDS
American Girls Abroad 186
The Greatest Moments of a Girl's Life 187
The Six Senses 188
Framed Postcards with Poems 189

5   POSTCARD BACKS
American 192
European 198

APPENDIX
Index 205
Price Guide & Collector's Checklist 209

Introduction

This reference book will provide readers with an amazing look at every American and European postcard, illustrated by Harrison Fisher, known to exist. Over 500 examples are shown in full color. Unusual treasures include: book, product, and theatre advertising postcards, rare American cards, overprints, variations, postcard panels, and European cards from Austria, Bulgaria, Finland, France, Germany, The Netherlands, Poland, and Russia. Other topics include postcards issued by the Detroit Publishing Company, and Reinthal & Newman's extensive line of cards.

From 1902 to 1910, Fisher illustrated at least fifteen book advertising postcards. During the postcard era, collector's overlooked book advertising postcards as a collectible topic, and often did not save these cards. The book advertising postcards promoted novels written by many well-known authors. The images usually appeared on the novel's dust jacket, book cover inlay, frontispiece, or on a bookplate. Publishers issued most book advertising postcards as a double card, with a perforation in the middle, designed to be torn off and returned to the publisher, or book store, to order the book. Most cards found today have the order portion removed, making the double cards elusive and considerably more valuable. The oldest Harrison Fisher postcard known to exist appears on a book advertising postcard for a novel written by Molly Elliott Seawell, titled *Francezka,* and published by Bowen-Merrill in 1902. The image on the postcard appears on a bookplate within the novel.

From 1904 to 1913, Fisher illustrated several product advertising postcards used to sell soap, sewing supplies, jewelry, and lithograph prints. His clients included Armour & Company, C.A. Swanson Jewelers, Warren Featherbone, and the United States Printing & Lithograph Company. These companies often used the images, appearing on the product advertising postcards, within their firm's advertising campaigns. For example, The Warren Featherbone Company, manufacturer of sewing supplies for women's clothing, used the image of *The Featherbone Girl,* shown on page 22, as a full-page advertisement within the September 1904 issue of *The Ladies' Home Journal* magazine. In 1906, Armour & Company, manufacturer of food and household products, issued a set of twelve product advertising postcards, titled *The American Girl Series,* that featured the girls of Karl Anderson, Walter Appleton Clark, John Cecil Clay, Howard Chandler Christy, Harrison Fisher, C. Allan Gilbert, Henry Hutt, Hamilton King, F.S. Manning, Thomas M. Pierce, W.T. Smedley, and G.G. Wiederseim. The postcard within this series, drawn by Harrison Fisher, appears on page 22 titled *The Harrison Fisher Girl.* Armour & Company printed the postcards in black and white, and distributed them within the United States and Germany. This postcard series, issued at the turn of the century, provides an early look at the American girl from several different artistic perspectives.

Postcards advertising actors and actresses for an appearance in a stage production are rare today, even in advanced collections. The only Fisher postcard known to exist in this category, shown on page 25, contains the title *Beverly Calhoun* which advertises George Barr McCutcheon's play, *Beverly of Graustark*, held at the Knickerbocker Theatre in New York. In 1904, Dodd, Mead originally published *Beverly of Graustark*, and Grosset & Dunlap reprinted the novel. The novel contains the image of *Beverly* on the book cover inlay and frontispiece. *Beverly's* image also appears on sheet music, calendar plates, china plates, bowls, and on a vase. Photographs of these unique items appear in *The Complete Works of Harrison Fisher* reference book.

In 1905, the Detroit Publishing Company acquired the rights to numerous *Life* magazine cartoons, and published them in their 14,000 series. The series includes the work of several illustrators: Harrison Fisher, James Montgomery Flagg, Charles Dana Gibson, Henry Hutt, Frederic Remington, and others. Harrison Fisher's illustrations appear on ten postcards within the 14,000 series, and appear on page 28. In 1902 and 1903, nine of the postcard images originally appeared as cartoons in the interior pages of *Life* magazine. *Life* published one image on the cover of their July 10, 1902 issue.

In 1906, Albert E. Reinthal and Stephen L. Newman established a firm bearing their name, Reinthal & Newman. Mr. Reinthal was president and Mr. Newman was the vice president and treasurer. Reinthal & Newman became one of the leading American art publishing houses noted for reproducing paintings of popular artists on postcards, prints, and for their fine art publications that included mezzotints and photogravures. They maintained an office in New York and a branch office in London, selling their products at wholesale prices to a variety of distributors within the United States and Europe. Reinthal & Newman issued nearly 300 postcards illustrated by Fisher which are featured in the content of this book. This number far exceeds any other illustrator within their portfolio, which testifies to Fisher's enormous popularity in the postcard era. Many early Reinthal & Newman postcards within the Unnumbered Series, Series 101, Series 102, and Series 103 contain a J. Beagles & Co. or Chas H. Hauff imprint on the back of the card. Both companies, located in London, sold the extensive line of postcards published by Reinthal & Newman which provided a worldwide market for their cards. Thus both their names as the British seller and that of Reinthal & Newman as the publisher are located on the address side. Wildt & Kray, another European distributor, reprinted the Unnumbered Series that contains twelve Fisher images. Postcards distributed by Wildt & Kray have their imprint and series number, 1488, printed on the back of a standard Reinthal & Newman postcard. For collectors who enjoy collecting number variations, the 1488 Series provides a challenge.

In order to protect the postcard images from overseas copyright infringement, Reinthal & Newman began to issue their cards with a Universal Copyright imprint or Entered Stationers Hall imprint on the back of their cards. Most examples seen today begin with Series 108 and continue through the English Reprint Series.

Reinthal & Newman utilized the printing services of several New York based companies including American Colortype, Quardi-Color, and the United States Lithograph & Printing Company. The United States Lithograph & Printing Company printed the water color postcard series—a printing process uniquely different from the traditional postcard presses.

The Cosmopolitan Print Department sold postcards published by Reinthal & Newman. These postcards contain the Cosmopolitan Print Department imprint along with a series letter printed on the back of the cards. Examples of the imprint and series letter appear in Reinthal & Newman Series 832-849, 860-877, and 970-979. Some cards exist with the imprint covered with a thick black line, and Reinthal & Newman's name printed below, but the series letter remained on the card. Examples of these imprint variations appear in Chapter 5 titled *Postcard Backs*.

For nine consecutive years, from 1914 through 1922, the Cosmopolitan Print Department issued catalogs featuring postcards of Harrison Fisher, Rolf Armstrong, Howard Chandler Christy, James Montgomery Flagg, Bessie Pease Gutmann, Jessie Wilcox Smith, Penrhyn Stanlaws, and many other well-known illustrators. Many of Fisher's images distributed by the Cosmopolitan Print Department originally appeared on the covers of their magazine. Sample pages of a 1919 catalog, shown on the following page, features Fisher's images first, and consume nearly half the catalog.

Records pertaining to the number of Harrison Fisher postcards issued by Reinthal & Newman do not exist. If rarity today is an indication, Reinthal & Newman apparently issued Series 400-423, Series 468-473, Series 600-617, and Series 970-979 in considerably smaller quantities. Specific images have also become scarce due to the volume of individuals who collect them. For example, Fisher's golf images attract golf memorabilia collectors, and others enjoy the pleasure of collecting Santa Claus', children, couples, animals, or tea cups. This provides Fisher collectors with a challenge in locating specific images to complete the entire collection of Harrison Fisher postcards.

Reinthal & Newman usually sold postcards in sets of six or twelve wrapped in a thin paper envelope that contained the title of the series. The title of the series appears on one of the postcards within the set, examples include: Series 101 *Danger,* Series 108 *Debutante,* Series 180-185 *Naughty, Naughty!,* Series 192-203 *In the Toils,* and Series 252-257 *Luxury.* Due to the rarity of postcard envelopes, collectors seldom see this unique item. Although Reinthal & Newman sold the majority of cards in sets of six or twelve, they issued the World War I Patriotic Series G, numbers 976-979, in a set of four. They

1919 Cosmopolitan Print Department Catalog

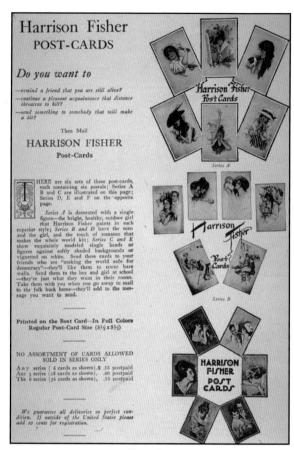

Page 9

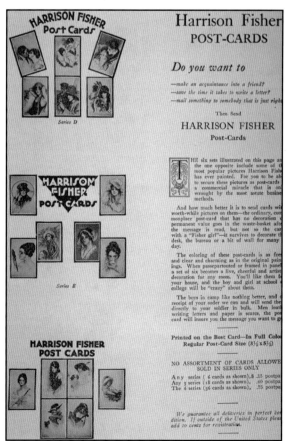

Page 10

Page 11

sold three postcard images individually, *The Kiss* postcard number 108, *Here's Happiness* postcard number 819, and *The Song of the Soul* postcard number 856.

Many of Fisher's images that Reinthal & Newman published on their postcards originally appeared on magazine covers for *American Sunday Monthly, Collier's, Cosmopolitan, Good Dressing, Good Housekeeping, The Ladies' Home Journal, The Ladies' World, Nash's, Pictorial Review, Puck, The Saturday Evening Post,* and *The Women's Home Companion.* For photographs of these covers refer to Chapter 5, titled *Magazine Cover Art,* within *The Complete Works of Harrison Fisher* reference book, which contains nearly 600 magazine cover images illustrated by Fisher.

For eight consecutive years, from 1907 to 1914, three publishers, Bobbs-Merrill, Charles Scribner's Sons, and Dodd, Mead published a total of fifteen art books illustrated by Fisher. Reinthal & Newman reprinted many of the images published in the art books on their postcards. Chapter 2, titled *Art Books by Harrison Fisher,* within *The Complete Works of Harrison Fisher* reference book provides photographs of the images within the art books.

Titles of images printed on postcards often varied from the titles used by the publisher's of magazines and art books. For example, Reinthal & Newman postcard number 764, titled *Close to Shore,* appears on a *Cosmopolitan* magazine cover titled *A Fair Breeze.* Reinthal & Newman postcard number 193, titled *Undue Haste,* appears in Fisher's art book, *The Little Gift Book,* titled *In Days of Old.* Numerous other examples of title variations exist, and are cited in the postcard descriptions.

The Greatest Moments of a Girl's Life series was one of the most popular set of postcards issued by Reinthal & Newman. The series contains six postcard images: *The Proposal, The Trousseau, The Wedding, The Honeymoon, The First Evening in Their Own Home,* and *Their New Love.* Reinthal & Newman issued the series with postcard numbers 186 through 191, but some extremely rare postcards contain numbers 468 through 473. Reinthal & Newman also issued the series mounted in a large rectangular frame commonly referred to as a postcard panel. Two different styles exist, one with the title of the image printed on a standard size postcard, and another with the title of the image printed on the mat below the postcard. Reinthal & Newman produced the postcard panel with three different titles: *The Greatest Moments of a Girl's Life, Life's Eventful Moments,* and *Six Important Events in a Girl's Life.* Chapter 4, titled *Framed Postcards,* shows a photograph of the postcard panels. Fisher originally drew the series for *The Ladies' Home Journal* magazine in 1911 titled *The Greatest Period in a Girl's Life.* Two of the images appear in full color on the cover of the *Journal,* and four appear in the interior pages as black and white illustrations. In 1912 and 1913, Charles Scribner's Sons reprinted the series in two of Fisher's art books, *American Girls in Miniature* and *A Girls Life and Other Pictures.*

Reinthal & Newman issued another popular series, titled *The Six Senses*. The series contains six postcard images: *Sense of Sight-The First Meeting, Sense of Smell-Falling in Love, Sense of Taste-Making Progress, Sense of Hearing-Anxious Moments, Sense of Touch-To Love and Cherish,* and *Common Sense-The Greatest Joy.* Reinthal & Newman issued the postcards as a water color series printed on an absorbent buff-colored card stock, with postcard numbers 700 through 705. They also issued the series as a postcard panel. In 1915, Fisher originally drew *The Six Senses* for the *American Sunday Monthly* magazine, a syndicated Sunday supplement, owned by William Randolph Hearst. Mr. Hearst inserted the supplement into six of his newspapers: *Atlanta American, Boston American, Chicago Examiner, Los Angeles Examiner, New York American,* and the *San Francisco Examiner.* Each image appears in full color on the cover of the supplement. The images never appeared in Fisher's art books. Dodd, Mead published the last Fisher art book, in 1914, one year before Fisher created *The Six Senses.*

A few rare Fisher postcards contain holiday greeting overprints. Publishers added overprints to postcards to increase sales during major holidays such as Easter, Christmas, and New Years. They printed the greetings in a variety of languages, English, Dutch, Finnish, German, and Swedish. Postcards with overprints have become increasingly difficult to locate, and increase the value of the card. Several overprint examples appear in Chapter 3 titled *Overprints & Variations.*

Harrison Fisher's European postcards provide collectors with another challenge. Chapter 2, titled *European Postcards,* features over 200 Austrian, Bulgarian, Danish, Finnish, French, German, Polish, and Russian postcards. Nearly thirty of these images never appeared on American postcards. The European issues have many unique characteristics not offered on American cards. Examples include hand colored and tinted postcards, real photo type postcards, sepia postcards, black & white postcards, and reversed images. Another example is novelty cards. Postcard manufacturers issued a wide variety of novelty cards in an attempt to increase sales, and to outwit their primary competitors. Publishers attached all sorts of items to the face of the cards. The most frequently encountered items include real hair, feathers, beads, and pieces of cloth. The only Fisher card known to exist in this category appears in the Finnish K.K. Oy. No 1/20 series, titled *Mistletoe,* featured on page 133. The card contains real hair and a red satin bow applied to the card.

As noted in the postcard descriptions, the author lists the name of the publisher or printer where known, but many European postcards do not have any source of identification. Generally, European postcards do not have the same quality of printing as enjoyed with the Reinthal & Newman issues, and it is much more difficult to obtain examples in excellent condition. Some of the European issues are practically non-existent, and are worth adding to ones collection in any reasonable condition.

CHAPTER ONE

American Postcards

Book Advertising Postcards

From 1902 to 1910, Harrison Fisher illustrated at least fifteen book advertising postcards to promote novels written by many well-known authors. The images used for these postcards usually appeared on the novel's dust jacket, book cover inlay, frontispiece, or on a bookplate. Most book advertising postcards were issued as a double card, with a perforation in the middle, designed to be torn off and returned to the publisher, or book store, to order the book. Most cards found today have the order portion removed, making the double cards elusive and more valuable. Advertising postcards are one of the rarest categories of American postcards Harrison Fisher ever illustrated.

54=40 or Fight (Not shown)
Novel written by Emerson Hough, and illustrated by Arthur Keller. Published by Bobbs-Merrill in 1909, and reprinted by Grosset & Dunlap.

The Bill-Toppers
Novel written and illustrated by Andre Castaigne. Published by Bobbs-Merrill in 1909, and reprinted by A.L. Burt. The image appears on the novel's dust jacket of both editions. The publisher printed the postcard in color.

Francezka (Not shown)
Novel written by Molly Elliott Seawell, and illustrated by Harrison Fisher. Published by Bowen-Merrill in 1902, and reprinted by Grosset & Dunlap. The image appears on a bookplate within the novel.

The Goose Girl
Novel written by Harold MacGrath, and illustrated by Andre Castaigne. Published by Grosset & Dunlap, circa 1909. The image appears on the novel's dust jacket and the book cover inlay. *The Ladies' Home Journal* magazine published the image on the cover of their December 1908 issue.

Half a Rouge (Not shown)
Novel written by Harold MacGrath, and illustrated by Harrison Fisher. Published by Bobbs-Merrill in 1906, and reprinted by Grosset & Dunlap. The image appears on the novel's book cover inlay and frontispiece, titled *Patty Bennington,* of both editions.

The Hungry Heart (Not shown)
Novel written by David Graham Phillips. Published by A.L. Burt in 1909. The image appears on the novel's dust jacket. *The Saturday Evening Post* magazine published the image on the cover of their June 13, 1908 issue.

Jane Cable
Novel written by George Barr McCutcheon, and illustrated by Harrison Fisher. Published by Dodd, Mead in 1906, and reprinted by A.L. Burt. The image appears on the novel's book cover inlay of both editions. The image appears in Fisher's art book, *The Harrison Fisher Book,* and on the cover of sheet music.

Jewell Weed (Not shown)
Novel written by Alice Ames Winter, and illustrated by Harrison Fisher. Published by Bobbs-Merrill in 1906, and reprinted by Grosset & Dunlap. The image appears on the novel's book cover inlay. *Madame* magazine published the image on the cover of their March 1906 issue.

The Man from Brodney's (Not shown)
Novel written by George Barr McCutcheon, and illustrated by Harrison Fisher. Published by Dodd, Mead in 1908, 1909, and 1916, and reprinted by Grosset & Dunlap. The image appears on the novel's book cover inlay.

My Commencement (Not shown)
Book advertising postcard for a souvenir book used by students to record memorable events of graduation. Published by Dodd, Mead in 1910. The image appears on the book's frontispiece. The image appears on a bookplate in Fisher's art book *A Garden of Girls*. *Cosmopolitan* magazine published the image on the cover of their February 1910 issue.

My Lady of Cleeve/You are the keeper of my heart
Novel written by Percy John Hartley, and illustrated by Herman Pfeifer. Published by Dodd, Mead in 1908 and 1909, and reprinted by A.L. Burt. The image appears on the novel's book cover inlay for all three editions. The image appears on a bookplate in Fisher's art book *Bachelor Belles*.

Nedra
Novel written by George Barr McCutcheon, and illustrated by Harrison Fisher. Published by Dodd, Mead in 1905 and 1907, and reprinted by Grosset & Dunlap. The image appears on the novel's book cover inlay for all three editions. The image appears on a bookplate in Fisher's art book, *The Harrison Fisher Book,* and on the cover of sheet music.

The One Way Out (Not shown)
Novel written by Bettina Von Hutten, and illustrated by Harrison Fisher. Published by Dodd, Mead in 1906, and reprinted by Grosset & Dunlap. The image appears on the novel's frontispiece for both editions. The image appears on a bookplate in Fisher's art book *The Harrison Fisher Book.*

The Stooping Lady (Not shown)
Novel written by Maurice Henry Hewlett, and illustrated by Harrison Fisher. Published by Dodd, Mead in 1907, and reprinted by A.L. Burt. The image appears on the novel's frontispiece for both editions. The image appears in Fisher's art book, *The Harrison Fisher Book,* titled *Ruth*. Reinthal & Newman reprinted the image on a postcard within the Unnumbered Series titled *Ruth*. *The Saturday Evening Post* magazine published the image on the cover of their January 12, 1907 issue.

The Title Market (Not shown)
Novel written by Emily Post, and illustrated by J.H. Gardner Soper. Published by A.L. Burt in 1909. The image appears on the novel's dust jacket illustrated by Harrison Fisher.

The Violet Book (Not shown)
Novel written by Bettina Von Hutten. No other information is available.

Book Advertising Postcard
The Bill-Toppers
Photo courtesy of Roy Nuhn

Book Advertising Postcard
The Goose Girl

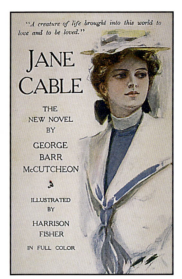
Book Advertising Postcard
Jane Cable

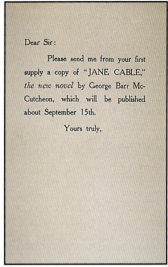
Reply Card
Jane Cable

Book Advertising Postcard
My Lady of Cleeve/You are
the keeper of my heart

Book Advertising Postcard
Nedra

Product Advertising Postcards

From 1904 to 1913, Harrison Fisher illustrated approximately four product advertising postcards to sell soap, sewing supplies, jewelry, and lithograph prints. Due to the rarity of product advertising postcards, others may exist that have not surfaced yet. His clients included Armour & Company, C.A. Swanson Jewelers, Warren Featherbone, and the U.S. Printing & Lithograph Company. For information regarding Harrison Fisher's commercial assignments, refer to Chapter 8, titled *Advertisements,* within *The Complete Works of Harrison Fisher* reference book.

The Featherbone Girl
Product advertising postcard for The Warren Featherbone Company–manufacturer of sewing supplies for women's clothing. During 1904 and 1905, the firm used the image of *The Featherbone Girl* in its advertising campaigns. *The Ladies' Home Journal* magazine published the image in their September 1904 issue as a full-page black and white advertisement.

The Fisher Girl
Product advertising postcard for C.A. Swanson & Company, Jewelers, 1202 Tower Ave, Superior, Wisconsin. The postcard contains a company logo with a swan in the middle of a rising sun. The image is untitled, and the reverse side of the postcard is blank. The same image exists on another product advertising postcard No. M6013, titled *The Fisher Girl,* and copyrighted in 1908 by Brown & Bigelow, St. Paul U.S.A.

Gathering Honey
Product advertising postcard for The U.S. Printing & Lithograph Company. The postcard promotes their printing services for art pictures, catalogs, labels, banners, and show-cards. Reinthal & Newman issued the same image on a postcard within the Water Color Series No. 392. Reinthal & Newman printed the postcard with the women's dress in two different colors, pink and green. The image appears in Fisher's art book, *Beauties,* with the woman's dress in pink. *Pictorial Review* magazine published the image on the cover of their October 1913 issue with the woman's dress in green. Reinthal & Newman used this postcard as part of the *Smiles and Kisses* postcard panel.

The Harrison Fisher Girl
Product advertising postcard for Armour & Company, manufacturer of food and household products. Armour & Company issued the postcard in black and white within the United States and Germany. The image on the German postcard is slightly smaller. During 1907, *The Harrison Fisher Girl* was used extensively in the firm's advertising campaigns, which included a 1907 company calendar. *Life* magazine published the image in their July 24, 1907 issue to promote the sales of Ponds Extract Soap.

22 HARRISON FISHER, ILLUSTRATOR

Product Advertising Postcard
The Featherbone Girl

Product Advertising Postcard
(The Fisher Girl)

Product Advertising Postcard
The Fisher Girl - variation

Product Advertising Postcard
Gathering Honey

Product Advertising Postcard
The Harrison Fisher Girl
United States

Product Advertising Postcard
The Harrison Fisher Girl
Germany

Rare American Postcards

As noted in the postcard descriptions, a variety of publishers issued the ten rare postcards featured below. Based on the rarity of these cards, the publishers probably issued the cards in smaller quantities as they are seldom seen by collectors today.

Untitled (As a beast I can destroy you and I will)
Published by Metropolitan Post Card Company. The postcard does not contain a title. The image and title appear on a bookplate for a novel written by George Barr McCutcheon, titled *Jane Cable*, and published by Dodd, Mead in 1906. The A.L. Burt reprint edition does not contain the postcard image.

Beverly Calhoun
Published by Kraus Manufacturing Company, New York, K. 1062. The back of the postcard advertises the play, *Beverly of Graustark*, held at the Knickerbocker Theatre in New York. The play was based on a novel written by George Barr McCutcheon, and published by Dodd, Mead in 1904. There were two printings of the postcard. One postcard is numbered K. 102 and the other K. 405. This postcard is the only Fisher theatre advertising postcard known to exist.

Untitled (Don't you know any better?)
Published by Tichnor Bros., Boston, Mass. No. 126984. The postcard does not contain a title. The image appears on the frontispiece for a novel written by George Barr McCutcheon, titled *Truxton King*, and published by Dodd, Mead in 1909. Grosset & Dunlap reprinted the novel.

Grace Vernon
Unknown Publisher. The image appears on a bookplate for a novel written by George Barr McCutcheon, titled *Nedra*, and published by Dodd, Mead in 1905 and 1907. Grosset & Dunlap reprinted the novel.

Untitled (The handsomest man of all was staring boldly at Jane's averted face)
Published by C.T. American Art (Curt Teich). The postcard does not contain a title. The image and title appear on a bookplate for a novel written by George Barr McCutcheon, titled *Jane Cable*, and published by Dodd, Mead in 1906. The A.L. Burt reprint edition does not contain the image.

His feeble glance took in her face with lifeless interest
Published by Frank V. Draper Co., Des Moines, IA. The image appears on a bookplate for a novel written by George Barr McCutcheon, titled *Jane Cable*, and published by Dodd, Mead in 1906. The A.L. Burt reprint edition contains the postcard image on the frontispiece.

Indian Maid
Published by The Albertype Co., Brooklyn, New York, circa 1921. The back of the postcard reads "Indian Maid Painted on Sandstone Rock by Harrison Fisher, Tassajara Hot Springs, Monterey County, California, Handcolored Post Card, The Finest American Made View Post Cards-The Albertype Co.,Brooklyn, N.Y." Another Indian Maiden postcard exists with a similar image. The Daley-Soeger Co., Printers, San Francisco published the card. The front of the card reads "Original oil painting of Indian Maiden by Harrison Fisher on natural rock at Tassajara Hot Springs."

Untitled (Jane Cable)
Published by H.G. Zimmerman, Chicago. The postcard image does not contain a title. The title of the image appears on the frontispiece for a novel written by George Barr McCutcheon, titled *Jane Cable,* and published by Dodd, Mead in 1906. The A.L. Burt reprint edition does not contain the image.

Untitled (Lady Tennys)
Published by C.T. American Art (Curt Teich) The postcard does not contain a title. The image and title appear on the frontispiece for a novel written by George Barr McCutcheon, titled *Nedra,* and published by Dodd, Mead in 1905 and 1907. The Grosset & Dunlap reprint edition contains the postcard image on the frontispiece.

To My Valentine (Not shown)
Unknown Publisher. Reinthal & Newman issued an image variation on postcard No. 193 titled *Undue Haste.* The variation contains a reversed image, and a grandfather clock in the background with different postcard colors. The image appears in two of Fisher's art books, *American Beauties* and *The Little Gift Book,* titled *In Days of Old.* The *Pictorial Review* magazine published the image on the cover of their January 1909 issue.

RARE AMERICAN POSTCARDS 25

(As a beast I can destroy . . .)
Metropolitan Post Card Co.

Beverly Calhoun
Kraus Mfg. Co.
From Carol Groesch's collection

(Don't you know any better?)
Tichnor Bros.

Grace Vernon
Unknown Publisher

(The handsomest man of all . . .)
C.T. American Art

His feeble glance took in . . .
Frank V. Draper Co.

Indian Maid
The Albertype Co.

(Jane Cable)
H.G. Zimmerman

(Lady Tennys)
C.T. American Art

Detroit Publishing Company

In 1905, the Detroit Publishing Company was formed–the oldest manufacturer of picture postcards. During the company's first year of operation, they issued the 14,000 series, and included ten postcards illustrated by Harrison Fisher. They originally printed the series with undivided backs, but when the postal requirements changed, on March 1, 1907, they issued divided backs in a smaller quantity. The majority of cards found today have undivided backs, with divided backs being more scarce.

Life magazine originally published the images as cartoons within the interior pages of their magazine. *Life* published one postcard image, number 14,039, on the cover of their magazine. The cards have a copyright date of 1902 or 1903, the year in which the cartoon received copyright through Life Publishing Company for publication in *Life* magazine. The Detroit Publishing Company printed the cards in sepia ink, and they printed card number 14,028 in sepia ink and black ink.

I don't see why you like me any better because I am changeable. Every time I kiss you it is like kissing another girl.
(Detroit No. 14,028)
Life magazine originally published the cartoon in their November 13, 1902 issue, page 414.

An Important Occasion. The groom: Our anniversary! What anniversary dearest? The bride (sadly): Have you forgotten so soon? We've been married a week to-day.
(Detroit No. 14,036)
Life magazine originally published the cartoon in their July 30, 1903 issue, page 101.

He: So you won't kiss and make up? Well, I won't make up.
(Detroit No. 14,037)
Life magazine originally published the cartoon in their April 17, 1902 issue, page 323. In 1902, Life Publishing Company published the cartoon in a book titled *The Social Comedy*. For more information refer to Chapter 3, titled *Art Books by Famous Illustrators,* within *The Complete Works of Harrison Fisher* reference book.

Between Themselves. He: You know you married me for my money. She: Well, I'm glad you give me credit for not being an utter fool.
(Detroit No. 14,038)
Life magazine originally published the cartoon in their July 17, 1902 issue, page 47.

Can't you give me your answer? It's cruel to keep me in suspense. But think of the length of time you have kept me in suspense.
(Detroit No. 14,039)
Life magazine originally published the cartoon on the cover of their July 10, 1902 issue.

I suppose you lost your heart to that Boston girl too. Not quite—but it was frost-bitten.
(Detroit No. 14,040)
Life magazine originally published the cartoon in their December 25, 1902 issue, page 561.

It's just horrid, Bertie, to think of living in a flat after we are married. You don't love me when you talk that way. Oh, yes, but not on a small scale.
(Detroit No. 14,041)
Life magazine originally published the cartoon in their February 6, 1902 issue, page 115.

Wasn't there any time while you were making love to me dear, that you were embarrassed? Oh yes! Just about the time when I was getting that ring.
(Detroit No. 14,042)
Life magazine originally published the cartoon in their January 1, 1903 issue, page 15.

He: And shall we never meet again? Never! Unless you want to come around occasionally and take me to luncheon or the matinee.
(Detroit No. 14,043)
Life magazine originally published the cartoon in their June 4, 1903 issue, page 523.

The caption: I fear there is no hope for us. We may sink at any moment. Seasick passenger: O lord! And I'm afraid it's fully two miles to the bottom.
(Detroit No. 14,044)
Life magazine originally published the cartoon in their September 4, 1902 issue, page 195.

28 HARRISON FISHER, ILLUSTRATOR

Detroit No. 14,028
I don't see why . . .

Detroit No. 14,036
An Important Occasion

Detroit No. 14,037
So you won't kiss . . .

Detroit No. 14,038
Between Themselves

Detroit No. 14,039
Can't you give me . . .

Detroit No. 14,040
I suppose you lost . . .

Detroit No. 14,041
It's just horrid . . .

Detroit No. 14,042
Wasn't there any . . .

Detroit No. 14,043
And shall we . . .

Detroit No. 14,044
I fear there is . . .

Unnumbered Series

The Unnumbered Series contains a set of twelve postcards issued by Reinthal & Newman. One of three publishers copyrighted the images: Charles Scribner's Sons, Curtis Publishing Company, or P.F. Collier & Son. The postcards contain copyright dates between 1905 and 1908. Reinthal & Newman reprinted five of the images with older copyright dates within Series 107: *American Beauties, A Fair Driver, Over the Teacup, A Thoroughbred,* and *Those Bewitching Eyes.*

Wildt & Kray, a European distributor of postcards for Reinthal & Newman, reprinted the entire Unnumbered series. Postcards issued by Wildt & Kray have their imprint, and Series No. 1488, printed on the back of the card. The Unnumbered Series and Series 1488 are the only Reinthal & Newman postcards that contain the words "Printed in U.S.A." inside the stamp box.

After the Dance (Unnumbered Series)
Copyright 1907 by the Curtis Publishing Company. The image appears in Fisher's art book *The Harrison Fisher Book*. *The Saturday Evening Post* magazine published the image on the cover of their February 2, 1907 issue.

American Beauties (Unnumbered Series)
Copyright 1907 by Charles Scribner's Sons. Reinthal & Newman reprinted the image, within Series 107, with an older copyright date of 1908. The image appears on two Finnish postcards, Real Photo Type Series and W. & G. American Series N:o 7001/1-35. The image also appears in two of Fisher's art books, *The American Girl* and *The Harrison Fisher Book*. *Success* magazine published the image as a full-page black and white illustration in their March 1908 issue.

The Critical Moment (Unnumbered Series)
Copyright 1905 by Charles Scribner's Sons. The image appears on a German postcard within the Alfred Schweizer/MEU Series. The image appears in Fisher's art book *The Harrison Fisher Book*. Reinthal & Newman also sold the postcard in a frame and printed the following information on the back of the frame, "Miniatures from Life, Harrison Fisher's Society Sketches, Hand Colored, Series No. 727."

A Fair Driver (Unnumbered Series)
Copyright 1907 by P.F. Collier & Son. Reinthal & Newman issued another postcard with a Christmas Greeting overprint. Reinthal & Newman reprinted the image, within Series 107, with an older copyright date of 1908 by Charles Scribner's Sons. The publishers printed the image in two colors, yellow and red. The image appears in two of Fisher's art books, *The American Girl* and *Fair Americans*. The image appears in the art book, *Thirty Favorite Paintings,* titled *How Pleasant It Is to Have Money*. *Collier's* magazine published the image, titled *The Little Heiress,* on the cover of their November 2, 1907 issue. Charles Scribner's Sons published the image in their 1909 Harrison Fisher Calendar.

The Motor Girl (Unnumbered Series)
Copyright 1908 by Charles Scribner's Sons. The image appears in two of Fisher's art books, *The American Girl* and *Fair Americans.* The image appears in *Thirty Favorite Paintings* titled *Ready for a Spin. Collier's* magazine published the image, titled *Ready for the Road,* on the cover of their May 9, 1908 issue. Charles Scribner's Sons published the image in their 1909 art calendar.

Over the Teacup (Unnumbered Series)
Copyright 1907 by Charles Scribner's Sons. Reinthal & Newman reprinted the image, within Series 107, with an older copyright date of 1908. Another postcard exists with a Christmas greeting overprint. The image appears in two of Fisher's art books, *The American Girl* and *The Harrison Fisher Book.*

Ready for the Run (Unnumbered Series)
Copyright 1907 by Charles Scribner's Sons. The image appears in Fisher's art book *The Harrison Fisher Book.*

Ruth (Unnumbered Series)
Copyright 1907 by the Curtis Publishing Company. In 1907, Dodd, Mead published the image on a book advertising postcard to promote the sales of a novel, *The Stooping Lady,* written by Maurice Henry Hewlett. A.L. Burt reprinted the novel. The image of *Ruth* appears on the frontispiece of both editions. The image appears in Fisher's art book *The Harrison Fisher Book.* *The Saturday Evening Post* magazine published the image on the cover of their January 12, 1907 issue.

A Tennis Champion (Unnumbered Series)
Copyright 1907 by Charles Scribner's Sons. Reinthal & Newman printed the image in two colors, red and yellow. The image appears in two of Fisher's art books, *The American Girl* and *The Harrison Fisher Book,* titled *The Champion.* *The Saturday Evening Post* magazine published the image on the cover of their May 25, 1907 issue.

A Thoroughbred (Unnumbered Series)
Copyright 1907 by Charles Scribner's Sons. Reinthal & Newman reprinted the image, within Series 107, with an older copyright date of 1908. The image appears on two Danish postcards, Uitgave Louis Diefenthal Series and Uitg. de Muinck Series No. R 193. The image appears in two of Fisher's art books, *The American Girl* and *The Harrison Fisher Book,* titled *A Blue-Ribbon Winner.* *The Saturday Evening Post* magazine published the image on the cover of their April 13, 1907 issue.

Those Bewitching Eyes (Unnumbered Series)
Copyright 1906 by Charles Scribner's Sons. Reinthal & Newman reprinted the image, within Series 107, with an older copyright date of 1908. The image appears on two Russian postcards, Rishar Series No. 117 and Linen Series No. 6. The image appears in two of Fisher's art books, *The American Girl* and *The Harrison Fisher Book.* The image appears on the book cover inlay for the art book titled *Pictures in Color by Famous American Artists.* *The Ladies' Home Journal* magazine published the image on the cover of their October 1907 issue.

The Winter Girl (Unnumbered)
Copyright 1907 by Charles Scribner's Sons. Reinthal & Newman issued the postcard with a New Years Greeting overprint. The image appears in Fisher's art book *The Harrison Fisher Book.* *The Saturday Evening Post* magazine published the image on the cover of their March 30, 1907 issue.

UNNUMBERED SERIES 31

Unnumbered Series
After the Dance

Unnumbered Series
American Beauties

Unnumbered Series
The Critical Moment

Unnumbered Series
A Fair Driver

Unnumbered Series
A Fair Driver
(with overprint & color variation)

Unnumbered Series
The Motor Girl

Unnumbered Series
Over the Teacup

Unnumbered Series
Over the Teacup
(with overprint)

Unnumbered Series
Ready for the Run

Unnumbered Series
Ruth

Unnumbered Series
A Tennis Champion

Unnumbered Series
A Tennis Champion
(color variation)

32 HARRISON FISHER, ILLUSTRATOR

Unnumbered Series
A Thoroughbred

Unnumbered Series
Those Bewitching Eyes

Unnumbered Series
The Winter Girl

Unnumbered Series
The Winter Girl
(with overprint)

Series 101 "Danger"

Series 101 contains a set of six postcards issued by Reinthal & Newman, and copyrighted by Charles Scribner's Sons in 1908. Reinthal & Newman issued the postcards with the series number, 101, printed on the back of each card: *Anticipation, Beauties, Danger, Odd Moments, The Old Miniature,* and *Reflections.*

In 1912, Reinthal & Newman issued six additional postcards: *American Beauties, A Fair Driver, Over the Teacup, The Study Hour, A Thoroughbred,* and *Those Bewitching Eyes.* All of the images, except *The Study Hour,* were previously issued within the Unnumbered Series. Reinthal & Newman issued these postcard reprints with Series 107 printed on the back of the card, but some examples have been seen without postcard numbers. The Series 107 reprints also contain older copyright dates of 1908, and contain the words "Printed in America" below the stamp box. Postcards containing these titles, but without postcard numbers belong to the Unnumbered Series if they contain copyright dates between 1906 and 1907. Also all postcards originally issued within the Unnumbered Series contain the words "Printed in U.S.A." inside the stamp box.

When Reinthal & Newman issued Series 107 New American Art Postcards combined the cards into Series 101 and 107, and sold the series as a set of 12 postcards titled "Danger." Since Reinthal & Newman originally issued each set of postcards with a different postcard series number, 101 and 107, they are listed and shown separately.

Anticipation (Series 101)
Copyright 1908 by Charles Scribner's Sons. The image appears in two of Fisher's art books, *American Girls in Miniature* and *Fair Americans. The Saturday Evening Post* magazine published the image on the cover of their December 12, 1908 issue. The image appears on a print titled *Under the Mistletoe.* Reinthal & Newman sold the postcard, mounted in a frame, with a poem under the image.

Beauties (Series 101)
Copyright 1908 by Charles Scribner's Sons. Reinthal & Newman reprinted the image within the English Reprint Series No. 2099. The image appears in three of Fisher's art books, *The American Girl, American Girls in Miniature,* and *Fair Americans.*

Danger (Series 101)
Copyright 1908 by Charles Scribner's Sons. Reinthal & Newman also sold the postcard in a frame with a poem underneath the image. For more information refer to Chapter 4 titled *Framed Postcards.* The image appears on a Danish postcard within the Uitg. de Muinck Series No. R 191. The image appears in two of Fisher's art books, *American Girls in Miniature* and *Fair Americans. Cosmopolitan* magazine published the image on the cover of their May 1909 issue.

Odd Moments (Series 101)
Copyright 1908 by Charles Scribner's Sons. Reinthal & Newman reprinted the image within the English Reprint Series No. 2100. The image appears in two of Fisher's art books, *American Girls in Miniature* and *Fair Americans.*

The Old Miniature (Series 101)
Copyright 1908 by Charles Scribner's Sons. Reinthal & Newman reprinted the image within the English Reprint Series No. 2098. Reinthal & Newman also sold the postcard in a frame with a poem underneath the image. For more information refer to the Chapter 4 titled *Framed Postcards*. The image appears in three of Fisher's art books, *The American Girl, American Girls in Miniature,* and *Fair Americans*. Charles Scribner's Sons printed the image on the cover of their 1909 Harrison Fisher Calendar.

Reflections (Series 101)
Copyright 1908 by Charles Scribner's Sons. The image appears in three of Fisher's art books, *American Girls in Miniature, Bachelor Belles,* and *Fair Americans*.

SERIES 101 35

Series 101
Anticipation

Series 101
Beauties

Series 101
Danger

Series 101
Odd Moments

Series 101
The Old Miniature

Series 101
Reflections

Series 102 "American Girls Abroad"

Series 102 contains a set of six postcards issued by Reinthal & Newman, and copyrighted by Charles Scribner's Sons in 1909. Reinthal & Newman issued the postcards with the series number, 102, printed on the back of each card.

In 1909, *The Ladies' Home Journal* magazine originally published the series, titled *American Girls Abroad,* as full-page black and white illustrations within their magazine. Charles Scribner's Sons reprinted the series in three of Fisher's art books, *American Girls in Miniature, Fair Americans,* and *Pictures in Color.* The series also appears on Danish postcards from The Netherlands, shown on page 120, titled *The Dollarprincess* instead of *The American Girl.*

The American Girl in Japan (Series 102)
Copyright 1909 by Charles Scribner's Sons. *The Ladies' Home Journal* magazine published the image in their May 1909 issue as the first illustration within the *American Girls Abroad* series.

The American Girl in England (Series 102)
Copyright 1909 by Charles Scribner's Sons. *The Ladies' Home Journal* magazine published the image in their June 1909 issue as the second illustration within the *American Girls Abroad* series.

The American Girl in Ireland (Series 102)
Copyright 1909 by Charles Scribner's Sons. *The Ladies' Home Journal* magazine published the image in their July 1909 issue as the third illustration within the *American Girls Abroad* series.

The American Girl in Italy (Series 102)
Copyright 1909 by Charles Scribner's Sons. *The Ladies' Home Journal* magazine published the image in their August 1909 issue as the fourth illustration within the *American Girls Abroad* series.

The American Girl in France (Series 102)
Copyright 1909 by Charles Scribner's Sons. *The Ladies' Home Journal* magazine published the image in their September 1909 issue as the fifth illustration within the *American Girls Abroad* series.

The American Girl in The Netherlands (Series 102)
Copyright 1909 by Charles Scribner's Sons. *The Ladies' Home Journal* magazine published the image in their October 1909 issue as the sixth and last illustration within the *American Girls Abroad* series. The image appears in two of Fisher's art books, *Fair Americans* and *Pictures in Color,* titled *The American Girl in Holland.*

SERIES 102   37

Series 102
The American Girl in Japan

Series 102
The American Girl in England

Series 102
The American Girl in Ireland

Series 102
The American Girl in Italy

Series 102
The American Girl in France

Series 102
The American Girl in The Netherlands

Series 103

Series 103 contains a set of six postcards issued by Reinthal & Newman, and copyrighted by Charles Scribner's Sons between 1904 and 1907. Reinthal & Newman issued the postcards with the series number, 103, printed on the back of each card. Reinthal & Newman reprinted the image, titled *The Canoe,* in Series 123 with an older copyright date of 1908.

In 1907, Charles Scribner's Sons originally published all of the images in Fisher's art book *The Harrison Fisher Book.* In 1910, they published one image, titled *Engagement Days,* in *Pictures in Color.*

An Hour with Art (Series 103)
Copyright 1904 by Charles Scribner's Sons. The image appears in Fisher's art book *The Harrison Fisher Book.*

The Canoe (Series 103)
Copyright 1904 by Charles Scribner's Sons. Reinthal & Newman published the same image on another postcard within Series 123 with an older copyright date of 1908. The image appears in Fisher's art book, *The Harrison Fisher Book,* titled *In the Canoe.*

Engagement Days (Series 103)
Copyright 1906 by Charles Scribner's Sons. The image appears in two of Fisher's art books, *The Harrison Fisher Book* titled *Not Yet-But Soon* and *Pictures in Color* titled *Engagement Days.*

Fisherman's Luck (Series 103)
Copyright 1907 by Charles Scribner's Sons. The image appears in Fisher's art book *The Harrison Fisher Book.*

Fore (Series 103)
Copyright 1907 by Charles Scribner's Sons. The image appears in Fisher's art book *The Harrison Fisher Book.*

Wanted-An Answer (Series 103)
Copyright 1907 by Charles Scribner's Sons. The image appears in Fisher's art book *The Harrison Fisher Book.*

SERIES 103   39

Series 103
An Hour with Art

Series 103
The Canoe

Series 103
Engagement Days

Series 103
Fisherman's Luck

Series 103
Fore

Series 103
Wanted-An Answer

Series 107 "Danger"

Series 107 contains a set of six postcards issued by Reinthal & Newman, and copyrighted by Charles Scribner's Sons in 1908. Reinthal & Newman issued the postcards with the series number, 107, printed on the back of each card.

Reinthal & Newman originally issued all of the images, except *The Study Hour*, within the Unnumbered Series. Postcards containing these titles with copyright dates between 1906 and 1907, and without a series number printed on the back of the card, belong to the Unnumbered Series. All postcards originally issued within the Unnumbered Series contain the words "Printed in U.S.A." inside the stamp box. All postcards within Series 107, except *Those Bewitching Eyes,* contain 1908 copyright dates, and the words "Printed in America" below the stamp box. Postcards with Series 107 printed on the back of the card are extremely difficult to locate.

American Beauties (Series 107)
Copyright 1908 by Charles Scribner's Sons. Reinthal & Newman published the image within the Unnumbered Series with an earlier copyright date of 1907. The image appears on two Finnish postcards, Real Photo Type Series and W. & G. American Series N:o 7001/1-35. The image appears in two of Fisher's art books, *The American Girl* and *The Harrison Fisher Book*. *Success* magazine published the image as a full-page black and white illustration in their March 1908 issue.

A Fair Driver (Series 107)
Copyright 1908 by Charles Scribner's Sons. Reinthal & Newman published the image within the Unnumbered Series with an earlier copyright date of 1907 by P.F. Collier & Son. The image appears in two of Fisher's art books, *The American Girl* and *Fair Americans.* The image appears in the art book, *Thirty Favorite Paintings,* titled *How Pleasant It Is to Have Money. Collier's* magazine published the image, titled *The Little Heiress,* on the cover of their November 2, 1907 issue.

Over the Teacup (Series 107)
Copyright 1908 by Charles Scribner's Sons. Reinthal & Newman published the image within the Unnumbered Series with an earlier copyright date of 1907. The image appears in two of Fisher's art books, *The American Girl* and *The Harrison Fisher Book.*

The Study Hour (Series 107)
Copyright 1908 by Charles Scribner's Sons. The image appears on a Danish postcard, within the Uitg. de Muinck Series No. R 192, titled *A Study Hour.* The image appears in two of Fisher's art books, *The American Girl* and *Fair Americans. The Ladies' Home Journal* magazine published the image in their April 1908 issue as a full-page black and white illustration, and part of the *College Girl* Series. For more information refer to Chapter 7, titled *Series,* within *The Complete Works of Harrison Fisher* reference book.

A Thoroughbred (Series 107)
Copyright 1908 by Charles Scribner's Sons. Reinthal & Newman published the image within the Unnumbered Series with an earlier copyright date of 1907. The image appears on two Danish postcards, Uitg. de Muinck Series No. R 193, titled *Thoroughbred,* and Uitgave Louis Diefenthal Series. The image appears in two of Fisher's art books, *The American Girl* titled *A Thoroughbred* and *The Harrison Fisher Book* titled *A Blue-Ribbon Winner.* *The Saturday Evening Post* magazine published the image on the cover of their April 13, 1907 issue.

Those Bewitching Eyes (Series 107)
Copyright by Charles Scribner's Sons. Reinthal & Newman published the image within the Unnumbered Series with an earlier copyright date of 1906. The image appears on two Russian postcards, Rishar Series No. 117 and Linen Series No. 6. The image appears in two of Fisher's art books, *The American Girl* and *The Harrison Fisher Book.* The image appears on the book cover inlay for an art book titled *Pictures in Color by Famous American Artists.* *The Ladies' Home Journal* magazine published the image on the cover of their October 1907 issue.

Series 107
American Beauties

Series 107
A Fair Driver

Series 107
Over the Teacup

Series 107
The Study Hour

Series 107
A Thoroughbred

Series 107
Those Bewitching Eyes

Series 108 "Debutante"

Series 108 contains a set of thirteen postcards issued by Reinthal & Newman, and copyrighted by Charles Scribner's Sons. Nine of the postcards contain a 1910 copyright date, and four postcards do not have copyright dates. The set originally contained six images with the series number, 108, printed on the back of each card, but some cards exist without the series number: *An Old Song, The Bride, The Debutante, Dumb Luck, His Gift,* and *Song of the Soul.* Reinthal & Newman added six more postcards to the series and titled the series *Debutante: The Ambush, The Artist, He's Only Joking, The Kiss, Lost?,* and *Oh! Promise Me.* The image, titled *Song of the Soul,* which Reinthal & Newman issued earlier received a different title, *The Artist,* creating twelve images on thirteen postcards.

The Ambush (Series 108)
Copyright 1910 by Charles Scribner's Sons. The image appears on a Danish postcard within the Uitg. de Muinck Series No. R 197. The image appears in two of Fisher's art books, *Fair Americans* and *Pictures in Color.* *The Ladies' Home Journal* magazine published the image as a full-page color illustration in their September 1909 issue.

An Old Song (Series 108)
Copyright 1910 by Charles Scribner's Sons. The image appears in two of Fisher's art books, *American Girls in Miniature* and *Fair Americans.* *The Saturday Evening Post* magazine published the image on the cover of their September 25, 1909 issue.

The Artist (Series 108)
Copyright by Charles Scribner's Sons. Reinthal & Newman issued another postcard with the same image in this series, but with a different title *Song of the Soul.* Later, Reinthal & Newman issued a third card with the same image, titled *The Song of the Soul,* and numbered the card 856. The image appears on a Danish postcard within the Uitg. de Muinck Series No. R 217. The image appears on a Bulgarian postcard within the Apollon Sophia Series titled *La Musique (Music).* The image appears in two of Fisher's art books, *American Girls in Miniature* titled *Song of the Soul* and *Fair Americans* titled *The Artist.* *The Ladies' Home Journal* magazine published the image in their August 1910 issue as a full-page black and white illustration, titled *The Musical Girl,* and part of *The Girls I Like Best* Series.

The Bride (Series 108)
Copyright 1910 by Charles Scribner's Sons. The image appears in two of Fisher's art books, *American Girls in Miniature* and *Fair Americans.* *The Ladies' Home Journal* magazine published the image on the cover of their October 1, 1910 issue. The image appears on a 1991 cross stitch pattern.

The Debutante (Series 108)
Copyright 1910 by Charles Scribner's Sons. The image appears on a Finnish postcard within the Titled Series titled *To Ball.* The image appears on a Russian postcard within the English Back Series, No. 15, titled *To Ball.* The image appears in three of Fisher's art books, *American Girls in Miniature, Fair Americans* (image variation), and *Pictures in Color* (image variation). *The Ladies' Home Journal* magazine published the image on the cover of their September 1, 1910 issue.

Dumb Luck (Series 108)
Copyright by Charles Scribner's Sons. The image appears on a Danish postcard within the Uitg. de Muinck Series No. R 188. The image appears in two of Fisher's art books, *The American Girl* and *Fair Americans*. *The Saturday Evening Post* magazine published the image on the cover of their November 28, 1908 issue.

He's Only Joking (Series 108)
Copyright 1910 by Charles Scribner's Sons. The image appears in two of Fisher's art books, *American Girls in Miniature* and *Fair Americans*. *The Saturday Evening Post* magazine published the image on the cover of their April 2, 1910 issue.

His Gift (Series 108)
Copyright 1910 by Charles Scribner's Sons. The image appears in two of Fisher's art books, *American Girls in Miniature* and *Fair Americans*. *The Saturday Evening Post* magazine published the image on the cover of their February 5, 1910 issue.

The Kiss (Series 108)
The postcard does not contain a copyright notice or copyright date. Reinthal & Newman issued another postcard containing an image variation within the English Reprint Series No. 2053. The same image variation appears on five European postcards: Danish-Uitg. de Muinck Series No. 186 R, Russian-Modern Art Sofia Series No. 024 (2), Russian-Sepia Series, and Russian-E.K. Series No 4. The image appears in three of Fisher's art books, *Fair Americans* (image variation), *A Girls Life and Other Pictures* (image variation), and *The Little Gift Book*. *The Ladies' Home Journal* magazine published the image on the cover of their July 1910 issue.

Lost? (Series 108)
Copyright 1910 by Charles Scribner's Sons. The image appears on a Danish postcard within the Uitg. de Muinck Series No. R 232. The image appears in two of Fisher's art books, *Fair Americans* and *Pictures in Color*.

Oh! Promise Me (Series 108)
Copyright 1910 by Charles Scribner's Sons. The image appears in two of Fisher's art books, *American Girls in Miniature* titled *Oh! Promise Me* and *Fair Americans* titled *Robin Adair*. *The Saturday Evening Post* magazine published the image on the cover of their January 15, 1910 issue.

Song of the Soul (Series 108)
Refer to: *The Artist*

Two Up (Series 108)
Copyright 1910 by Charles Scribner's Sons. The image appears in two of Fisher's art books, *American Girls in Miniature* and *Fair Americans*. *The Ladies' Home Journal* magazine published the image on the cover of their November 1909 issue.

SERIES 108   45

Series 108
The Ambush

Series 108
An Old Song

Series 108
The Artist

Series 108
The Bride

Series 108
The Debutante

Series 108
Dumb Luck

Series 108
He's Only Joking

Series 108
His Gift

Series 108
The Kiss

Series 108
Lost?

Series 108
Oh! Promise Me

Series 108
Song of the Soul

Series 108
Two Up

Series 123

Series 123 contains a set of six postcards issued by Reinthal & Newman, and copyrighted by Charles Scribner's Sons between 1905 and 1908. Reinthal & Newman printed the series number, 123, on the back of each card, but some cards exist without the series number. The author includes an additional postcard, titled *The Fudge Party*, only because the title appears in other postcard books as being part of the series. The author has not seen *The Fudge Party* with Series 123 printed on the back of the card, and cannot positively identify the card as being part of the series. Reinthal & Newman may have issued *The Fudge Party* as part of another series because the image does not contain the same theme as the other cards within the series. All other cards have a man and a woman included in the image, and *The Fudge Party* does not.

The Canoe (Series 123)
Copyright 1908 by Charles Scribner's Sons. Reinthal & Newman issued the image on another postcard, within Series 103, with an earlier copyright date of 1904. The image appears in Fisher's art book, *The Harrison Fisher Book*, titled *In the Canoe*.

The Fudge Party (Series 123?)
Copyright 1908 by Charles Scribner's Sons. *The Ladies' Home Journal* magazine published the image in their August 1908 issue as a full-page black and white illustration, and part of a series, titled *College Girls*. Two months later, in October 1908, *The Ladies' Home Journal* published the same image on the cover of the *Journal*. The image appears in two of Fisher's art books, *Fair Americans* and *Pictures in Color*.

In Clover (Series 123)
Copyright 1905 by Charles Scribner's Sons. The image appears in Fisher's art book *The Harrison Fisher Book*.

Making Hay (Series 123)
Copyright 1905 by Charles Scribner's Sons. The image appears in Fisher's art book *The Harrison Fisher Book*.

A Modern Eve (Series 123)
Copyright 1906 by Charles Scribner's Sons. The image appears on a Danish postcard within the Uitg. de Muinck Series No. R 221. The image appears in two of Fisher's art books, *The Harrison Fisher Book* and *Pictures in Color*.

Taking Toll (Series 123)
Copyright 1906 by Charles Scribner's Sons. The image appears in two of Fisher's art books, *The Harrison Fisher Book* and *Pictures in Color*.

You Will Marry a Dark Man (Series 123)
Copyright 1906 by Charles Scribner's Sons. The image appears on a Danish postcard within the Uitg. de Muinck Series No. R 233. The image appears in two of Fisher's art books, *The Harrison Fisher Book* and *Pictures in Color*.

48 HARRISON FISHER, ILLUSTRATOR

Series 123
The Canoe

Series 123 ?
The Fudge Party

Series 123
In Clover

Series 123
Making Hay

Series 123
A Modern Eve

Series 123
Taking Toll

Series 123
You Will Marry a Dark Man

Series 180-185 "Naughty, Naughty!"

Series 180-185 contains a set of six postcards issued by Reinthal & Newman. Three of the postcards contain a copyright notice by Reinthal & Newman, and three postcards contain a copyright notice by Charles Scribner's Sons. The postcards do not have copyright dates. Reinthal & Newman issued a postcard number on the back of each card, and reprinted three of the images within the English Reprint Series: *Following the Race, The Rose,* and *Well Protected.* As noted in the postcard descriptions the image, titled *The Rose,* appears on two pieces of sheet music, *For You a Rose Song* and *You Withered My Roses of Love.* Photographs of the sheet music appear in Chapter 10, titled *Sheet Music,* within *The Complete Works of Harrison Fisher* reference book.

Well Protected (No. 180)
Copyright by Reinthal & Newman. Reinthal & Newman issued the image on another postcard within the English Reprint Series No. 2090. The image appears on a Finnish postcard within the Titled Series titled *To Walk*. The image appears on two Russian postcards, English Back Series No. 23 titled *To Walk* and the Sepia Series. The image appears in four of Fisher's art books, *American Girls in Miniature, Beauties, Fair Americans,* and *A Girls Life and Other Pictures.* *The Ladies' Home Journal* magazine published the image on the cover of their February 1913 issue.

The Rose (No. 181)
Copyright by Reinthal & Newman. Reinthal & Newman issued the image on another postcard within the English Reprint Series No. 2089. The image appears on a Finnish postcard within the Titled Series, and on two Russian postcards, English Back Series No. 17 and AWE Real Photo Type Series. The image appears in two of Fisher's art books, *American Girls in Miniature* titled *The Rose* and *Fair Americans* titled *The Christmas Rose.* *The Saturday Evening Post* magazine published the image on the cover of their December 24, 1910 issue. This popular image appears on the cover of two pieces of sheet music, *For You a Rose Song* and *You Withered My Roses of Love.*

Miss Santa Claus (No. 182)
Copyright by Charles Scribner's Sons. The image appears on a Russian postcard within the AWE Real Photo Type Series. The image appears in three of Fisher's art books, *American Girls in Miniature, Fair Americans,* and *A Girls Life and Other Pictures.* *Cosmopolitan* magazine published the image on the cover of their January 1911 issue. *Nash's* magazine published the image on the cover of their February 1911 issue.

Miss Knickerbocker (No. 183)
Copyright by Reinthal & Newman. The image appears on a Finnish postcard within the Titled Series titled *A Dane.* The image appears on two Russian postcards, English Back Series No. 12 titled *A Dane* and AWE Real Photo Type Series. The image appears in three of Fisher's art books, *American Girls in Miniature, Fair Americans,* and *A Girls Life and Other Pictures.* *Cosmopolitan* magazine published the image on the cover of their November 1909 issue.

Following the Race (No. 184)
Copyright by Charles Scribner's Sons. The image appears on a Reinthal & Newman postcard within the English Reprint Series No. 2088. The image appears on four Finnish postcards, W. & G. American Series N:o 7001/1-35, Publisher at Polyphot American Series, No Identification Series, and within the Titled Series titled *Sport*. The image appears on a Russian postcard within the English Back Series No. 24 titled *Sport*. The image appears in two of Fisher's art books, *American Girls in Miniature* and *Fair Americans*. *The Saturday Evening Post* magazine published the image on the cover of their November 5, 1910 issue.

Naughty, Naughty! (No. 185)
Copyright by Charles Scribner's Sons. The image appears on an Austrian postcard distributed by B.K.W.I. The image appears in three of Fisher's art books, *American Girls in Miniature*, *Fair Americans* titled *Rejected* (image variation), and *A Girls Life and Other Pictures* (image variation) titled *Rejected*. *Cosmopolitan* magazine published the image variation on the cover of their May 1911 issue.

SERIES 180-185   51

No. 180
Well Protected

No. 181
The Rose

No. 182
Miss Santa Claus

No. 183
Miss Knickerbocker

No. 184
Following the Race

No. 185
Naughty, Naughty!

Series 186-191 "The Greatest Moments of a Girl's Life"
Series 468-473

The Greatest Moments of a Girl's Life series contains two sets of six postcards. Reinthal & Newman issued the first set with postcard numbers 186-191 printed on the back of each card. The second set contains postcard numbers 468-473 printed on the back of each card. Charles Scribner's Sons copyrighted the cards within both sets, but they do not contain copyright dates. The images also appear on Danish postcards from The Netherlands within the Uitg. de Muinck Series shown on page 116-119.

In 1911, *The Ladies' Home Journal* magazine originally published the series titled *The Greatest Period in a Girl's Life*. Two images, *The Wedding* and *Their New Love,* appear in full color on the cover of the *Journal,* and four images appear as full-page black and white illustrations within the *Journal.*

Charles Scribner's Sons reprinted the series in two of Fisher's art books, *American Girls in Miniature* published in 1912 and *A Girls Life and Other Pictures* published in 1913. In 1913, when Charles Scribner's Sons published the art book, *A Girls Life and Other Pictures,* they changed the title of the series to *The Greatest Moments of a Girl's Life.*

In addition to selling postcards, and reprinting the images in art books, Reinthal & Newman sold the series of cards in a large rectangular frame commonly referred to as a postcard panel. Two different styles exist, one with the title of the image printed on a standard size postcard, and another with the title of the image printed on the mat below the postcard. The framed sets have three different titles, *The Greatest Moments of a Girl's Life, Life's Eventful Moments,* and *Six Important Events in a Girl's Life.* Photographs of the postcard panels appear on page 187.

An unusual item that is rarely seen is a set of four prints mounted on a single mat and enclosed in a frame. The title of the series, *The Greatest Moments in a Girl's Life,* appears on the mat below the prints. The prints measure 6" x 8 3/4". The two images, from the series, that were not included in the set of prints are *The Honeymoon* and *Their New Love.* Another rare and unusual collectible item, from this series, is a miniature set of six prints mounted in individual metal frames measuring 1 1/2" x 2 1/2". These items are rarely encountered by collectors, even in advanced collections.

It is popular among collectors to collect several complete sets of the postcards from this series, one for their postcard collection, and another set to frame and enjoy within their home. Many collectors also frame a set as a wedding gift for a family member or friend. As a result it is difficult to locate postcards within the series, especially ones in excellent condition.

The Proposal (No. 186 & No. 468)
Copyright by Charles Scribner's Sons. The image appears on a Danish postcard within the Uitg de Muinck Series No. R 223. The image appears in two of Fisher's art books, *American Girls in Miniature* and *A Girl's Life and Other Pictures*. *The Ladies' Home Journal* magazine published the image as a full-page black and white illustration, within their March 15, 1911 issue, titled *The Supreme Moment-The Proposal.*

The Trousseau (No. 187 & No. 469)
Copyright by Charles Scribner's Sons. The image appears in two of Fisher's art books, *American Girls in Miniature* and *A Girl's Life and Other Pictures*. *The Ladies' Home Journal* magazine published the image as a full-page black and white illustration within their April 15, 1911 issue.

The Wedding (No. 188 & No. 470)
Copyright by Charles Scribner's Sons. The image appears in two of Fisher's art books, *American Girls in Miniature* and *A Girl's Life and Other Pictures*. *The Ladies' Home Journal* magazine published the image on the cover of their May 15, 1911 issue.

The Honeymoon (No. 189 & No. 471)
Copyright by Charles Scribner's Sons. The image appears on a Danish postcard within the Uitg. de Muinck Series No. R 224. The image appears in two of Fisher's art books, *American Girls in Miniature* and *A Girl's Life and Other Pictures*. *The Ladies' Home Journal* magazine published the image as a full-page black and white illustration within their July 1911 issue.

The First Evening in Their Own Home (No. 190 & No. 472)
Copyright by Charles Scribner's Sons. The image appears on a Danish postcard within the Uitg. de Muinck Series No. R 225. The image appears in two of Fisher's art books, *American Girls in Miniature* and *A Girl's Life and Other Pictures*. *The Ladies' Home Journal* magazine published the image as a full-page black and white illustration within their August 1911 issue.

Their New Love (No. 191 & No. 473)
Copyright by Charles Scribner's Sons. The image appears on a Danish postcard within the Uitg. de Muinck Series No. R 226. The image appears in two of Fisher's art books, *American Girls in Miniature* and *A Girl's Life and Other Pictures*. *The Ladies' Home Journal* magazine published the image on the cover of their October 1911 issue. Reinthal & Newman sold the image on a print, mounted in a frame, with a poem under the print titled *Mother.*

No. 186 & 468
The Proposal

No. 187 & 469
The Trousseau

No. 188 & 470
The Wedding

No. 189 & 471
The Honeymoon

No. 190 & 472
The First Evening in Their Own Home

No. 191 & 473
Their New Love

Series 192-203 "In the Toils"

Series 192-203 contains a set of twelve postcards issued and copyrighted by Reinthal & Newman. The postcards do not contain copyright dates. Reinthal & Newman issued a postcard number on the back of each card. Reinthal & Newman reprinted five images within the American Reprint Series or the English Reprint Series: *Cherry Ripe*, *Vanity*, *Beauties*, *And Yet Her Eyes Can Look Wise*, and *Maid, to Worship*.

In 1909, Bobbs-Merrill originally published all of the images in Fisher's art book *American Beauties*. In 1913, Charles Scribner's Sons reprinted all of the images in *The Little Gift Book*. As noted in the postcard descriptions many of the images in *The Little Gift Book* contain different titles than those printed on the postcards.

The image, titled *In the Toils,* appears on a unique and elusive item—a candy box made of cardboard with a high quality paper overlay. The candy box contained Fry Chocolates manufactured by J.S. Fry & Sons Limited located in Great Britain. A photograph of the candy box appears in Chapter 14, titled *Candy Boxes & Tins,* within *The Complete Works of Harrison Fisher* reference book.

Cherry Ripe (No. 192)
Copyright by Reinthal & Newman. Reinthal & Newman reprinted the image within the American Reprint Series No. 1001. The image appears on two Russian postcards, Linen Series No. 60 and Rishar Series No. 835. The image appears in two of Fisher's art books, *American Beauties* and *The Little Gift Book,* titled *Off to the Theatre.* The *Saturday Evening Post* magazine published the image on the cover of their April 17, 1909 issue.

Undue Haste (No. 193)
Copyright by Reinthal & Newman. The image appears in two of Fisher's art books, *American Beauties* and *The Little Gift Book,* titled *In Days of Old.* *Pictorial Review* magazine published the image on the cover of their January 1909 issue.

Sweetheart (No. 194)
Copyright by Reinthal & Newman. The image appears in two of Fisher's art books, *American Beauties* and *The Little Gift Book,* titled *Youth.* The *Saturday Evening Post* magazine published the image on the cover of their May 8, 1909 issue. The image appears on a collectible reproduction print advertising the Schlitz Brewing Company.

Vanity (No. 195)
Copyright by Reinthal & Newman. Reinthal & Newman reprinted the image within the American Reprint Series No. 1003. The image appears on three Russian postcards, Rishar Series No. 834, Linen Series No. 54, and AWE Real Photo Type Series. The image appears in two of Fisher's art books, *American Beauties* and *The Little Gift Book.* *Pictorial Review* magazine published the image on the cover of their October 1908 issue.

Beauties (No. 196)
Copyright by Reinthal & Newman. Reinthal & Newman reprinted the image within the American Reprint Series No. 1002. The image appears on a Russian postcard within the AWE Real Photo Type Series. The image appears on another Russian postcard issued by Frolov and Shourek, Moscow. The image appears in two of Fisher's art books, *American Beauties* and *The Little Gift Book.*

Lips for Kisses (No. 197)
Copyright by Reinthal & Newman. The image appears on two Russian postcards, Linen Series No. 72 and Rishar Series No. 833. The image appears in two of Fisher's art books, *American Beauties* and *The Little Gift Book,* titled *Lady with the Fan. The Saturday Evening Post* magazine published the image on the cover of their February 6, 1909 issue.

Bewitching Maiden (No. 198)
Copyright by Reinthal & Newman. The image appears on two Russian postcards, Linen Series No. 71 and Rishar Series No. 836. The image appears in two of Fisher's art books, *American Beauties* and *The Little Gift Book,* titled *Maud Muller. The Ladies' Home Journal* magazine published the image on the cover of their May 1908 issue.

Leisure Moments (No. 199)
Copyright by Reinthal & Newman. Reinthal & Newman reprinted the image on postcard No. 768. The image appears on three Russian postcards, Linen Series No. 2, Rishar Series No. 826, and Black & White Series. The image appears in two of Fisher's art books, *American Beauties* and *The Little Gift Book. The Saturday Evening Post* magazine published the image on the cover of their November 7, 1908 issue.

And Yet Her Eyes Can Look Wise (No. 200)
Copyright by Reinthal & Newman. Reinthal & Newman reprinted the image within the American Reprint Series No. 1005. The image appears on two Russian postcards, Linen Series No. 1 and Rishar Series No. 829. The image appears in two of Fisher's art books, *American Beauties* and *The Little Gift Book,* titled *The Eyes Under the Cowl.*

Roses (No. 201)
Copyright by Reinthal & Newman. The image appears on a Russian postcard within the AWE Real Photo Type Series. The image appears in two of Fisher's art books, *American Beauties* and *The Little Gift Book.*

In the Toils (No. 202)
Copyright by Reinthal & Newman. The image appears on a Russian postcard within the Rishar Series No. 825. The image appears in two of Fisher's art books, *American Beauties* and *The Little Gift Book. Cosmopolitan* magazine published the image on the cover of their March 1909 issue. The image appears on the lid of a candy box manufactured by J.S. Fry & Sons Limited located in Great Britain.

Maid, to Worship (No. 203)
Copyright by Reinthal & Newman. Reinthal & Newman reprinted the image within the American Reprint Series No. 1004. The image appears on a Russian postcard within the Rishar Series No. 824. The image appears in two of Fisher's art books, *American Beauties* and *The Little Gift Book . The Saturday Evening Post* magazine published the image on the cover of their October 10, 1908 issue.

SERIES 192-203   57

No. 192
Cherry Ripe

No. 193
Undue Haste

No. 194
Sweetheart

No. 195
Vanity

No. 196
Beauties

No. 197
Lips for Kisses

No. 198
Bewitching Maiden

No. 199
Leisure Moments

No. 200
And Yet Her Eyes Can Look Wise

No. 201
Roses

No. 202
In the Toils

No. 203
Maid, to Worship

Series 252-257 "Luxury"

Series 252-257 contains a set of six postcards issued and copyrighted by Reinthal & Newman. The postcards do not contain copyright dates. Reinthal & Newman issued a postcard number on the back of each card, but some cards exist without a postcard number. A credit line "Painted by Harrison Fisher" appears on the front of each card. Reinthal & Newman reprinted two images within the English Reprint Series, *Preparing to Conquer* and *Love Lyrics*. From 1911 to 1913, Charles Scribner's Sons published the images in Fisher's art books, *A Girls Life and Other Pictures, Fair Americans,* and/or *The Little Gift Book.*

Dreaming of You (No. 252)
Copyright by Reinthal & Newman. The image appears on a Russian postcard within the E.K. Series No. 25. The image appears in Fisher's art book, *The Little Gift Book,* titled *The Siesta.*

Luxury (No. 253)
Copyright by Reinthal & Newman. The image appears on a Russian postcard within the AWE Real Photo Type Series. The image appears in two of Fisher's art books, *A Girl's Life and Other Pictures* and *The Little Gift Book.* Charles Scribner's Sons published the image in their 1913 art calendar.

Pals (No. 254)
Copyright by Reinthal & Newman. The image appears in two of Fisher's art books, *Beauties* and *The Little Gift Book. Cosmopolitan* magazine published the image on the cover of their August 1912 issue titled *Diana. Nash's* magazine published the image on the cover of their September 1912 issue.

Homeward Bound (No. 255)
Copyright by Reinthal & Newman. The image appears on a Finnish postcard within the Titled Series. The image appears on three Russian postcards, Sepia Series, AWE Real Photo Type Series, and English Back Series. The image appears in two of Fisher's art books, *Maidens Fair* and *The Little Gift Book. The Saturday Evening Post* magazine published the image on the cover of their July 15, 1911 issue.

Preparing to Conquer (No. 256)
Copyright by Reinthal & Newman. Reinthal & Newman reprinted an image variation within the English Reprint Series No. 2051. The image appears on a Finnish postcard within the Titled Series and on a Russian postcard within the English Back Series No. 14. The image appears in three of Fisher's art books, *American Belles* (variation), *Fair Americans* titled *Behind the Scenes* (variation), and *The Little Gift Book* titled *The Make-Up. The Saturday Evening Post* magazine published the image on the cover of their October 22, 1910 issue.

Love Lyrics (No. 257)
Copyright by Reinthal & Newman. Reinthal & Newman reprinted the image within the English Reprint Series No. 2040. The image appears on two Finnish postcards, No. 30/25 Series and within the Titled Series. The image appears on a Russian postcard within the English Back Series The image appears in two of Fisher's art books, *The Little Gift Book* and *Maidens Fair. The Saturday Evening Post* magazine published the image on the cover of their August 5, 1911 issue.

SERIES 252-257 59

No. 252
Dreaming of You

No. 253
Luxury

No. 254
Pals

No. 255
Homeward Bound

No. 256
Preparing to Conquer

No. 257
Love Lyrics

Series 258-263 "Beauty"

Series 258-263 contains a set of six postcards issued and copyrighted by Reinthal & Newman. The postcards do not contain copyright dates. Reinthal & Newman issued a postcard number on the back of each card, but some cards exist without a postcard number. A credit line "Painted by Harrison Fisher appears on the front of each card. Reinthal & Newman reprinted four images within the American Reprint Series: *Good Night!*, *Girlie*, *Beauty and Value*, and *A Prairie Belle*. In 1913, Charles Scribner's Sons published all of the images in Fisher's art book *The Little Gift Book*.

Tempting Lips (No. 258)
Copyright by Reinthal & Newman. The image appears in two of Fisher's art books, *Fair Americans* titled *A Study* and *The Little Gift Book* titled *The Girl with the Red Feather*. *Cosmopolitan* magazine published the image on the cover of their March 1911 issue.

Good Night! (No. 259)
Copyright by Reinthal & Newman. Reinthal & Newman reprinted the image within the English Reprint Series No. 2102. The image appears on a Finnish postcard within the Titled Series, and on a Russian postcard within the English Back Series No. 19. The image appears in Fisher's art book *The Little Gift Book*. *Cosmopolitan* published the image on the cover of their November 1912 issue.

Bows Attract Beaus (No. 260)
Copyright by Reinthal & Newman. The image appears on a Russian postcard within the Sepia Series. The image appears in two of Fisher's art books, *American Belles* and *The Little Gift Book*. *Cosmopolitan* magazine published the image on the cover of their July 1911 issue.

Girlie (No. 261)
Copyright by Reinthal & Newman. Reinthal & Newman reprinted the image, within the English Reprint Series No. 2047, titled *Good Little Indian*. The image appears on a Finnish postcard within the W. & G. American Series N:o 7001/36-50. The image appears in two of Fisher's art books, *The Little Gift Book* titled *The School Girl* and *Maidens Fair*. *Cosmopolitan* magazine published the image on the cover of their March 1912 issue. The Cosmopolitan Print Dept. sold the image on a print titled *Babette*.

Beauty and Value (No. 262)
Copyright by Reinthal & Newman. Reinthal & Newman reprinted the image within the English Reprint Series No. 2049. The image appears on a Finnish postcard within the N$\underline{o}$. 30/25 Series. The image appears in two of Fisher's art books, *Beauties* and *The Little Gift Book*, titled *The College Girl*. The *Saturday Evening Post* magazine published the image on the cover of their June 29, 1912 issue.

A Prairie Belle (No. 263)
Copyright by Reinthal & Newman. Reinthal & Newman reprinted the image within the English Reprint Series No. 2103. The image appears on a Finnish postcard within the Titled Series and on a Russian postcard within the English Back Series No. 25. The image appears in two of Fisher's art books, *American Belles* and *The Little Gift Book*. The *Saturday Evening Post* magazine published the image on the cover of their December 10, 1910 issue.

SERIES 258-263   61

No. 258
Tempting Lips

No. 259
Good Night!

No. 260
Bows Attract Beaus

No. 261
Girlie

No. 262
Beauty and Value

No. 263
A Prairie Belle

Series 300-305 "Auto"

Series 300-305 contains a set of six postcards issued and copyrighted by Reinthal & Newman. The postcards do not contain copyright dates. Reinthal & Newman issued the cards with a postcard number printed on the back of each card, but some cards exist without a postcard number. A credit line "Painted by Harrison Fisher" appears on the front of each card. Reinthal & Newman reprinted the image, titled *Behave!*, within the English Reprint Series.

Auto Kiss (No. 300)
Copyright by Reinthal & Newman. The image appears in two of Fisher's art books, *Fair Americans* titled *On the Road* and *The Little Gift Book* titled *Touring? Cosmopolitan* magazine published the image on the cover of their September 1910 issue.

Sweethearts Asleep (No. 301)
Copyright by Reinthal & Newman. The image appears on a Russian postcard within the E.K. Series N<u>o</u> 3. The image appears in Fisher's art book, *The Little Gift Book,* titled *Playmates. The Ladies' Home Journal* magazine published the image as a full-page color illustration, titled *Asleep,* within their October 1912 issue.

Behave! (No. 302)
Copyright by Reinthal & Newman. Reinthal & Newman reprinted the image within the English Reprint Series No. 2045. The image appears on a Finnish postcard within the Titled Series titled *Be Hove!* The image appears in two of Fisher's art books, *The Little Gift Book* titled *Happy Moments* and *Maidens Fair*.

All Mine! (No. 303)
Copyright by Reinthal & Newman. Reinthal & Newman issued postcard No. 835 with the same title, but with a different image. The image appears on a Finnish postcard within the N<u>o</u>. 30/25 Series. The image appears in Fisher's art book *The Little Gift Book*. The image appears on a print titled *Sonny Boy*. *Cosmopolitan* magazine published the image on the cover of their September 1912 issue.

Thoroughbreds (No. 304)
Copyright by Reinthal & Newman. The image appears on a Finnish postcard within the K.K. Oy. N:o 1/20 Series. The image appears in two of Fisher's art books, *The Little Gift Book* and *Maidens Fair*. *The Saturday Evening Post* magazine published the image on the cover of their February 17, 1912 issue. The image appears on an art print titled *Good Fellowship*.

The Laugh Is on You! (No. 305)
Copyright by Reinthal & Newman. The image appears in two of Fisher's art books, *The Little Gift Book* and *Maidens Fair*.

SERIES 300-305 63

No. 300
Auto Kiss

No. 301
Sweethearts Asleep

No. 302
Behave!

No. 303
All Mine!

No. 304
Thoroughbreds

No. 305
The Laugh Is on You!

Water Color Series 381-386

Series 381-386 is the first water color series illustrated by Harrison Fisher. The postcards are copyrighted by Reinthal & Newman, but do not contain copyright dates. The series contains six postcards printed on an absorbent buff-colored card stock. Reinthal & Newman issued a postcard number on the back of each card. A variation of the image, titled *All's Well,* appears on candy tins manufactured by The Tin Decorating Company (Tindeco). Photographs of the candy tins appear in Chapter 14, titled *Candy Boxes & Tins,* within *The Complete Works of Harrison Fisher* reference book. As noted in the postcard descriptions below, Reinthal & Newman used two of the postcards, within this series, as part of the *Smiles and Kisses* postcard panel.

All's Well (No. 381)
Copyright by Reinthal & Newman. The image appears on two Finnish postcards, Otto Andersin Series and Real Photo Type Series. *Cosmopolitan* magazine published the image on the cover of their September 1913 issue. *Nash's* magazine published the image on the cover of their October 1913 issue. A variation of the image appears on candy tins, manufactured by The Tin Decorating Company (Tindeco), titled *The Yachting Girl.*

Two Roses (No. 382)
Copyright by Reinthal & Newman. The image appears on a Finnish postcard within the No. 30/25 Series. *Cosmopolitan* magazine published the image on the cover of their August 1913 issue. *Nash's* magazine published the image on the cover of their September 1913 issue.

Contentment (No. 383)
Copyright by Reinthal & Newman. Reinthal & Newman reprinted the image within the English Reprint Series No. 2050. The image appears on a Finnish postcard within the No Identification Series. *Cosmopolitan* magazine published the image on the cover of their February 1913 issue.

Not Yet-But Soon (No. 384)
Copyright by Reinthal & Newman. The image appears on a Finnish postcard within the No. 30/25 Series. *Cosmopolitan* magazine published the image on the cover of their January 1913 issue. The Cosmopolitan Print Department issued the image on a print titled *Impending.* Reinthal & Newman used this postcard as part of the *Smiles and Kisses* postcard panel.

Smile, Even if It Hurts! (No. 385)
Copyright by Reinthal & Newman. *Cosmopolitan* magazine published the image on the cover of their October 1913 issue. *Nash's* magazine published the image on the cover of their November 1913 issue. Reinthal & Newman used this postcard as part of the *Smiles and Kisses* postcard panel.

Speak! (No. 386)
Copyright by Reinthal & Newman. The image appears in Fisher's art book *Beauties. The Ladies' Home Journal* magazine published the image, titled *The Girl and the Cockatoo,* on the cover of their April 1913 issue.

SERIES 381-386   65

No. 381
All's Well

No. 382
Two Roses

No. 383
Contentment

No. 384
Not Yet-But Soon

No. 385
Smile, Even if It Hurts!

No. 386
Speak!

Water Color Series 387-392

Series 387-392 contains a set of six water color postcards printed on an absorbent buff-colored card stock. The postcards are copyrighted by Reinthal & Newman, but do not contain copyright dates. Reinthal & Newman issued a postcard number on the back of each card. Reinthal & Newman reprinted the image, titled *Undecided,* within the English Reprint Series. As noted in the postcard descriptions, the U.S. Printing & Lithograph Company reprinted the image, titled *Gathering Honey,* on a product advertising postcard to promote their services. Reinthal & Newman used four of the postcards, within the series, as part of the *Smiles and Kisses* postcard panel.

Welcome Home! (No. 387)
Copyright by Reinthal & Newman. The image appears on two Finnish postcards, N̲o̲. 30/25 Series (image variation) and the Numbered Series N:o 13. A variation of the image appears in Fisher's art book *Beauties*. *Cosmopolitan* magazine published the image on the cover of their April 1913 issue. Reinthal & Newman used this postcard as part of the *Smiles and Kisses* postcard panel.

A Helping Hand (No. 388)
Copyright by Reinthal & Newman. *Cosmopolitan* magazine published the image on the cover of their July 1913 issue. Reinthal & Newman used this postcard as part of the *Smiles and Kisses* postcard panel.

Undecided (No. 389)
Copyright by Reinthal & Newman. Reinthal & Newman reprinted the image within the English Reprint Series No. 2044. The image appears in Fisher's art book *Beauties*. Reinthal & Newman used this postcard as part of the *Smiles and Kisses* postcard panel.

Well Guarded (No. 390)
Copyright by Reinthal & Newman. The image appears in Fisher's art book *Beauties*.

My Lady Waits (No. 391)
Copyright by Reinthal & Newman. The image appears in Fisher's art book *Beauties*.

Gathering Honey (No. 392)
Copyright by Reinthal & Newman. Reinthal & Newman issued two postcards with the women's dress in different colors, pink and green, as shown on the following page. The U.S. Printing & Lithograph Company printed the image on a product advertising postcard to promote their services. A photograph of the product advertising postcard appears on page 22. The image appears in Fisher's art book *Beauties*. *Pictorial Review* magazine published the image on the cover of their October 1913 issue. Reinthal & Newman used this postcard as part of the *Smiles and Kisses* postcard panel.

SERIES 387-392   67

No. 387
Welcome Home!

No. 388
A Helping Hand

No. 389
Undecided

No. 390
Well Guarded

No. 391
My Lady Waits

No. 392
Gathering Honey

No. 392
Gathering Honey
(color variation)

Series 400-423

Series 400-423 contains a set of twenty-four postcards issued and copyrighted by Reinthal & Newman. The postcards do not contain copyright dates. Reinthal & Newman issued a postcard number on the back of each card. A credit line "Painted by Harrison Fisher" appears on the front of each card. The cards within this series are more difficult to locate, and demand higher market values. Reinthal & Newman reprinted ten images within the English Reprint Series: *The Pink of Perfection, He Won't Bite-, Refreshments, Princess Pat, Isn't He Sweet, Can't You Speak?, Ready and Waiting, The Parasol, Mary,* and *Courting Attention.*

Looking Backward (No. 400)
Copyright by Reinthal & Newman. Reinthal & Newman also sold the postcard in a frame and printed the following information on the back of the frame, "Miniatures from Life, Harrison Fisher's Society Sketches, Hand Colored, Series No. 727". The image appears in Fisher's art book *American Belles. The Saturday Evening Post* magazine published the image on the cover of their May 27, 1911 issue.

Art and Beauty (No. 401)
Copyright by Reinthal & Newman. The image appears in Fisher's art book *American Belles.*

The Chief Interest (No. 402)
Copyright by Reinthal & Newman. The image appears in Fisher's art book *A Garden of Girls. Cosmopolitan* magazine published the image on the cover of their April 1910 issue.

Passing Fancies (No. 403)
Copyright by Reinthal & Newman. The image appears on a Finnish postcard within the Titled Series titled *Bubbles.* The image appears on a Russian postcard within the English Back Series No. 9 titled *Bubbles.* The image appears in Fisher's art book *A Garden of Girls. Cosmopolitan* magazine published the image on the cover of their August 1909 issue.

The Pink of Perfection (No. 404)
Copyright by Reinthal & Newman. Reinthal & Newman reprinted the image within the English Reprint Series No. 2086. The image appears on a Finnish postcard within the Titled Series titled *A Beauty.* The image appears on a Russian postcard within the English Back Series titled *A Beauty.* The image appears in Fisher's art book *American Belles.*

He Won't Bite- (No. 405)
Copyright by Reinthal & Newman. Reinthal & Newman reprinted the image within the English Reprint Series No. 2087. The image appears on a Finnish postcard within the Titled Series titled *Friends.* The image appears on a Russian postcard within the English Back Series No. 7 titled *Friends.* The image appears in Fisher's art book *American Girls in Miniature. Cosmopolitan* magazine published the image on the cover of their August 1911 issue.

Refreshments (No. 406)
Copyright by Reinthal & Newman. Reinthal & Newman reprinted the image within the English Reprint Series No. 2096. The image appears in Fisher's art book *American Belles*. *Cosmopolitan* magazine published the image on the cover of their June 1911 issue.

Princess Pat (No. 407)
Copyright by Reinthal & Newman. Reinthal & Newman reprinted the image within the English Reprint Series No. 2046. The image appears on a Finnish postcard within the Titled Series. The image appears on four Russian postcards, Sepia Series, Real Photo Type Series No. 3223, English Back Series No. 20, and the No Identification Series. The image appears in Fisher's art book *A Garden of Girls*. *The Saturday Evening Post* magazine published the image on the cover of their May 21, 1910 issue. *Good Dressing* magazine published the image on the cover of their May 1913 issue.

Fine Feathers (No. 408)
Copyright by Reinthal & Newman. The image appears on a Russian postcard within the Sepia Series. The image appears in Fisher's art book *American Belles*.

Isn't He Sweet? (No. 409)
Copyright by Reinthal & Newman. Reinthal & Newman reprinted the image within the English Reprint Series No. 2097. The image appears on a Finnish postcard within the Titled Series titled *To Walk*. The image appears on two Russian postcards, English Back Series No. 2 and Sepia Series. The image appears in Fisher's art book *A Garden of Girls*. *The Saturday Evening Post* magazine published the image on the cover of their August 28, 1909 issue.

Maid at Arms (No. 410)
Copyright by Reinthal & Newman. The image appears on three Russian postcards, Real Photo Type Series, Sepia Series, and E.K. Series No. 19. The image appears in Fisher's art book *A Garden of Girls*.

He Cometh Not (No. 411)
Copyright by Reinthal & Newman. The image appears in Fisher's art book *A Garden of Girls*. *Cosmopolitan* magazine published the image on the cover of their October 1909 issue.

Can't You Speak! (No. 412)
Copyright by Reinthal & Newman. Reinthal & Newman reprinted the image within the English Reprint Series No. 2042. The image appears in Fisher's art book *American Belles*.

What Will She Say? (No. 413)
Copyright by Reinthal & Newman. The image appears in Fisher's art book *A Garden of Girls*.

Music Hath Charms (No. 414)
Copyright by Reinthal & Newman. The image appears in Fisher's art book *A Garden of Girls*.

Do I Intrude? (No. 415)
Copyright by Reinthal & Newman. The image appears in Fisher's art book *A Garden of Girls*. *The Saturday Evening Post* magazine published the image on the cover of their December 11, 1909 issue. *Vogue* magazine published the image, titled *Human Butterflies*, within their November 13, 1909 issue.

My Queen (No. 416)
Copyrighted by Reinthal & Newman. The image appears in Fisher's art book *A Garden of Girls*.

My Lady Drives (No. 417)
Copyright by Reinthal & Newman. The image appears on a Russian postcard within the Sepia Series. The image appears in Fisher's art book *American Belles*. The image appears on the frontispiece of a novel, titled *The Essential Thing*, written by Arthur Hodges and published by Dodd, Mead in 1912. The frontispiece is titled *Doris*.

Ready and Waiting (No. 418)
Copyright by Reinthal & Newman. Reinthal & Newman reprinted the image within the English Reprint Series No. 2092. The image appears on a Russian postcard within the English Back Series No. 22. The image appears in Fisher's art book *American Belles*.

The Parasol (No. 419)
Copyright by Reinthal & Newman. Reinthal & Newman reprinted the image within the English Reprint Series No. 2093. The image appears in Fisher's art book *American Belles*. *Cosmopolitan* magazine published the image on the cover of their December 1910 issue. The image appears on an art print, published by The Ullman Manufacturing Company, titled *Pensive Thoughts*.

Tempting Lips (No. 420)
Copyright by Reinthal & Newman. The image appears in Fisher's art book *American Belles*. *The Saturday Evening Post* magazine published the image on the cover of their February 4, 1911 issue.

Mary (No. 421)
Copyright by Reinthal & Newman. Reinthal & Newman reprinted the image within the English Reprint Series No. 2095. The image appears on a Russian postcard within the Sepia Series. The image appears in Fisher's art book *American Belles*. *The Saturday Evening Post* magazine published the image on the cover of their April 8, 1911 issue.

Courting Attention (No. 422)
Copyright by Reinthal & Newman. Reinthal & Newman reprinted the image within the English Reprint Series No. 2094. The image appears on a Russian postcard within the Sepia Series. The image appears in Fisher's art book *A Garden of Girls*. The image appears on a print titled *Her Infinite Variety*.

My Pretty Neighbor (No. 423)
Copyright by Reinthal & Newman. The image appears on a Russian postcard within the Sepia Series. The image appears in Fisher's art book *A Garden of Girls*.

SERIES 400-423

No. 400
Looking Backward

No. 401
Art and Beauty

No. 402
The Chief Interest

No. 403
Passing Fancies

No. 404
The Pink of Perfection

No. 405
He Won't Bite-

No. 406
Refreshments

No. 407
Princess Pat

No. 408
Fine Feathers

No. 409
Isn't He Sweet?

No. 410
Maid at Arms

No. 411
He Cometh Not

HARRISON FISHER, ILLUSTRATOR

No. 412
Can't You Speak?

No. 413
What Will She Say?

No. 414
Music Hath Charms

No. 415
Do I Intrude?

No. 416
My Queen

No. 417
My Lady Drives

No. 418
Ready and Waiting

No. 419
The Parasol

No. 420
Tempting Lips

No. 421
Mary

No. 422
Courting Attention

No. 423
My Pretty Neighbor

Series 600-617

Series 600-617 contains a set of eighteen postcards issued and copyrighted by Reinthal & Newman. The postcards do not contain copyright dates. Reinthal & Newman issued a postcard number on the back of each card. The postcards within this series are as difficult to locate as the cards within the previous 400-423 Series, and demand higher market values. Reinthal & Newman reprinted seven of the images within the English Reprint Series: *The Serenade, Good Morning Mama, A Fair Exhibitor, Paddling Their Own Canoe, Tea Time, Sketching,* and *Chocolate*.

A Winter Sport (No. 600)
Copyright by Reinthal & Newman. The image appears on a Polish postcard within the Polish and Ukrainian Back Series. The image appears in Fisher's art book *Beauties*. *Pictorial Review* magazine published the image on the cover of their January 1913 issue.

Winter Whispers (No. 601)
Copyright by Reinthal & Newman. The image appears on a Polish postcard within the Polish and Ukrainian Back Series. *The Ladies' World* magazine published the image on the cover of their January 1913 issue.

A Christmas "Him" (No. 602)
Copyright by Reinthal & Newman. An image variation (reversed image) appears in Fisher's art book, *A Girls Life and Other Pictures,* titled *A Happy New Year*. Charles Scribner's Sons published an image variation (reversed image) on the cover of their 1913 Harrison Fisher art calendar.

A Sprig of Holly (No. 603)
Copyright by Reinthal & Newman. The image appears on a Polish postcard within the Polish and Ukrainian Back Series. An image variation (without holly) appears on two Finnish postcards, Publisher at Polyphot American Series and W.&G. American Series N:o 7001/36-50. *Cosmopolitan* magazine published an image variation (without holly) on the cover of their November 1913 issue. *Nash's* magazine published the image on the cover of their December 1913 issue.

Snowbirds (No. 604)
Copyright by Reinthal & Newman. The image appears in Fisher's art book *American Belles*.

A Christmas Belle (No. 605)
Copyright by Reinthal & Newman. The image does not appear on another source.

The Serenade (No. 606)
Copyright by Reinthal & Newman. Reinthal & Newman reprinted the image within the English Reprint Series No. 2043 titled *Serenade*. Another English Reprint postcard exists with a German Happy New Year overprint. The image appears in Fisher's art book *Beauties*. *The Ladies' Home Journal* magazine published the image on the cover of their August 1913 issue. The image appears on a 1915 Harrison Fisher calendar titled *I Love You Best*.

The Secret (No. 607)
Copyright by Reinthal & Newman. The image appears on a bookplate for a novel written by George Barr McCutcheon, titled *The Alternative,* and published by Dodd, Mead and William Briggs in 1909. A.L. Burt reprinted the novel, and the image appears in all three editions.

Good Morning, Mamma (No. 608)
Copyright by Reinthal & Newman. Reinthal & Newman reprinted the image within the English Reprint Series No. 2076.

A Passing Glance (No. 609)
Copyright by Reinthal & Newman. The image appears in Fisher's art book *Maidens Fair*. *Women's Home Companion* magazine published the image on the cover of their March 1912 issue.

A Fair Exhibitor (No. 610)
Copyright by Reinthal & Newman. Reinthal & Newman reprinted the image within the English Reprint Series No. 2041. The image appears in Fisher's art book *Maidens Fair*. *Women's Home Companion* magazine published the image on the cover of their August 1911 issue.

Paddling Their Own Canoe (No. 611)
Copyright by Reinthal & Newman. Reinthal & Newman reprinted the image within the English Reprint Series No. 2069. A variation of the image appears in Fisher's art book *Beauties*. *The Ladies' Home Journal* magazine published the image variation on the cover of their August 1912 issue, and on a tin waste paper basket manufactured by Cheinco Housewares.

Tea Time (No. 612)
Copyright by Reinthal & Newman. Reinthal & Newman reprinted the image within the English Reprint Series No. 2101. *Cosmopolitan* magazine published the image on the cover of their December 1913 issue.

The Favorite Pillow (No. 613)
Copyright by Reinthal & Newman. The image appears on a Finnish postcard within the W. & G. American Series N:o 7001/36-50. *Cosmopolitan* magazine published the image on the cover of their June 1912 issue.

Don't Worry (No. 614)
Copyright by Reinthal & Newman. The image appears on a Finnish postcard within the Publisher at Polyphot American Series. *Cosmopolitan* magazine published the image on the cover of their March 1913 issue, and sold the image on a print titled *R.S.V.P.*

June (No. 615)
Copyright by Reinthal & Newman. The image appears on two Finnish postcards, Titled Series and Real Photo Type Series. The image appears on a Russian postcard within the English Back Series No. 10. The image appears in Fisher's art book *Beauties*. *Cosmopolitan* magazine published the image on the cover of their July 1912 issue. *Nash's* magazine published the image on the cover of their August 1912 issue.

Sketching (No. 616)
Copyright by Reinthal & Newman. Reinthal & Newman reprinted the image within the English Reprint Series No. 2091. *Cosmopolitan* magazine published the image on the cover of their April 1914 issue.

Chocolate (No. 617)
Copyright by Reinthal & Newman. Reinthal & Newman reprinted the image within the English Reprint Series No. 2048. The image appears in Fisher's art book *Maidens Fair*. *The Saturday Evening Post* magazine published the image on the cover of their January 20, 1912 issue.

No. 600
A Winter Sport

No. 601
Winter Whispers

No. 602
A Christmas "Him"

No. 603
A Sprig of Holly

No. 604
Snowbirds

No. 605
A Christmas Belle

No. 606
The Serenade

No. 607
The Secret

No. 608
Good Morning, Mamma

No. 609
A Passing Glance

No. 610
A Fair Exhibitor

No. 611
Paddling Their Own Canoe

SERIES 600-617   77

No. 612
Tea Time

No. 613
The Favorite Pillow

No. 614
Don't Worry

No. 615
June

No. 616
Sketching

No. 617
Chocolate

Water Color Series 700-705 "The Six Senses"

Water Color Series 700-705 contains a set of six water color postcards printed on an absorbent buff-colored card stock. The postcards are copyrighted by Reinthal & Newman, but do not contain copyright dates. Reinthal & Newman issued a postcard number on the back of each card. It is difficult to locate cards within the series, especially ones in excellent condition, as the absorbent buff-colored card stock often shows foxing. In addition to selling postcards, Reinthal & Newman sold the series of cards in a large rectangular frame commonly referred to as a postcard panel. Two different styles exist, one with the title of the image printed on a standard size postcard, and another with the title of the image printed on the mat below the postcard. A photograph of the postcard panel appears on page 188.

In 1915, Fisher originally drew *The Six Senses* for the *American Sunday Monthly* magazine, a syndicated Sunday supplement, owned by William Randolph Hearst. Mr. Hearst inserted the supplement into six of his newspapers: *Atlanta American, Boston American, Chicago Examiner, Los Angeles Examiner, New York American,* and the *San Francisco Examiner*. Each image appears in full color on the cover of the supplement. The covers are featured in Chapter 5, titled *Sunday Newspaper Supplements,* within *The Complete Works of Harrison Fisher* reference book.

Sense of Sight-The First Meeting (No. 700)
Copyright by Reinthal & Newman. *American Sunday Monthly* magazine published the image, titled *Seeing,* on the cover of their February 1915 issue.

Sense of Smell-Falling in Love (No. 701)
Copyright by Reinthal & Newman. *American Sunday Monthly* magazine published the image, titled *Smelling,* on the cover of their April 1915 issue.

Sense of Taste-Making Progress (No. 702)
Copyright by Reinthal & Newman. *American Sunday Monthly* magazine published the image, titled *Tasting,* on the cover of their March 1915 issue.

Sense of Hearing-Anxious Moments (No. 703)
Copyright by Reinthal & Newman. *American Sunday Monthly* magazine published the image, titled *Hearing,* on the cover of their January 1915 issue.

Sense of Touch-To Love and Cherish (No. 704)
Copyright by Reinthal & Newman. *American Sunday Monthly* magazine published the image, titled *Feeling,* on the cover of their May 1915 issue.

Common Sense-The Greatest Joy (No. 705)
Copyright by Reinthal & Newman. *American Sunday Monthly* magazine published the image, titled *Commonsense,* on the cover of their June 1915 issue.

SERIES 700-705   79

No. 700
Sense of Sight-The First Meeting

No. 701
Sense of Smell-Falling in Love

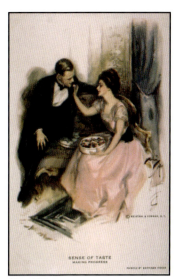

No. 702
Sense of Taste-Making Progress

No. 703
Sense of Hearing-Anxious Moments

No. 704
Sense of Touch-To Love and Cherish

No. 705
Common Sense-The Greatest Joy

Series 762-767

Series 762-767 contains a set of six postcards issued and copyrighted by Reinthal & Newman. The postcards do not contain copyright dates. Reinthal & Newman issued a postcard number on the back of each card. A credit line "Painted by Harrison Fisher" appears on the front of each card. The words "Printed in America" or "Printed in England" appears below the stamp box. The majority of cards found today contain the words "Printed in England". In 1915, *Cosmopolitan* originally published all of the images on the covers of their magazine.

Alone at Last (No. 762)
Copyright by Reinthal & Newman. Reinthal & Newman issued another postcard with the same postcard number that contains an image variation (without mistletoe) as shown on the following page. The same image variation (without mistletoe) appears on a Finnish postcard within the Real Photo Type Series. *Cosmopolitan* magazine published the image (with mistletoe) on the cover of their January 1915 issue. *Nash's* magazine published the image on the cover of their March 1915 issue.

Alert (No. 763)
Copyright by Reinthal & Newman. The image appears on a Finnish postcard within the W. & G. American Series N:o 7001/1-35. *Cosmopolitan* magazine published the image on the cover of their October 1915 issue.

Close to Shore (No. 764)
Copyright by Reinthal & Newman. The image appears on four Finnish postcards, N̲o̲. 30/25 Series, Numbered Series N:o 4, Pain. Karjalan Kirjap Series N:o 4, and Otto Andersin Series. *Cosmopolitan* and *Nash's* magazines published the image, titled *A Fair Breeze,* on the cover of their August 1915 issue.

Looks Good to Me (No. 765)
Copyright by Reinthal & Newman. *Cosmopolitan* magazine published the image, titled *Vanity,* on the cover of their May 1915 issue.

Passers By (No. 766)
Copyright by Reinthal & Newman. *Cosmopolitan* magazine published the image on the cover of their March 1915 issue. *Nash's* magazine published the image, titled *Dimples,* on the cover of their May 1915 issue.

At the Toilet (No. 767)
Copyright by Reinthal & Newman. The image appears on three Finnish postcards, Numbered Series N:o 11, W. & G. American Series N:o 7001/1-35, and Publisher at Polyphot American Series. *Cosmopolitan* and *Nash's* magazines published the image, titled *Good-morning!,* on the cover of their November 1915 issue.

SERIES 762-767   81

No. 762
Alone at Last

No. 762
Alone at Last
(image variation)

No. 763
Alert

No. 764
Close to Shore

No. 765
Looks Good to Me

No. 766
Passers By

No. 767
At the Toilet

Series 768-773

Series 768-773 contains a set of six postcards issued and copyrighted by Reinthal & Newman. The postcards do not contain copyright dates. Reinthal & Newman issued a postcard number on the back of each card. The words "Printed in America" or "Printed in England" appears below a standard size, solid line stamp box. The majority of cards found today contain the words "Printed in England". Additional postcards emerged with German captions printed directly below the postcard title. These cards have elongated broken line stamp boxes. As noted in the postcard descriptions two of these cards, titled *Drifting* and *Her Favorite "Him"*, contain different postcard numbers than their counterparts with solid line stamp boxes.

The author includes an additional postcard, titled *Leisure Moments,* postcard number 768, because the card contains a postcard number variation within this series. Reinthal & Newman originally issued the card within a previous series, and numbered the card 199.

Leisure Moments (No. 768)
Copyright by Reinthal & Newman. Reinthal & Newman originally issued the postcard within Series 192-203, and numbered the card 199. The image appears on three Russian postcards, Linen Series No. 2, Rishar Series No. 826, and the Black & White Series. The image appears in two of Fisher's art books, *American Beauties* and *The Little Gift Book*. *The Saturday Evening Post* magazine published the image on the cover of their November 7, 1908 issue.

Drifting (No. 768 & 769)
Copyright by Reinthal & Newman. The postcards numbered 768 contain the words "Printed in America", or "Printed in England" below a standard size solid line stamp box. The postcards numbered 769 contain an elongated broken line stamp box, and some examples contain a German caption printed directly under the postcard title. According to the Catalogue of Copyright Entries, Reinthal & Newman originally issued postcard No. 768 as *Drifting*. Reinthal & Newman reprinted the image within the American Reprint Series No. 1000. The image appears on two Finnish postcards, Real Photo Type Series and Otto Andersin Series. *American Sunday Monthly* magazine published the image on the cover of their June 1914 issue.

Her Favorite "Him" (No. 768 & 769)
Copyright by Reinthal & Newman. The postcards numbered 768 contain an elongated broken line stamp box, and/or a German caption. The postcards numbered 769 contain the words "Printed in America", or "Printed in England" below a standard size solid line stamp box. According to the Catalogue of Copyright Entries, Reinthal & Newman issued postcard No. 769 as *Her Favorite "Him"*. The image appears in Fisher's art book *Harrison Fisher Girls*. *The Ladies' Home Journal* magazine published the image on the cover of their March 1914 issue.

The Third Party (No. 770)
Copyright by Reinthal & Newman. The image appears in Fisher's art book *Harrison Fisher Girls*. *The Ladies' Home Journal* magazine published the image on the cover of their August 1914 issue. In the early 1980's, *The Ladies' Home Journal* magazine celebrated their 100th birthday, and sold reproductions of the image on round tin beer trays. For a photograph of the beer tray refer to Chapter 19, titled *Collectible Reproductions,* within *The Complete Works of Harrison Fisher* reference book.

Inspiration (No. 771)
Copyright by Reinthal & Newman. Reinthal & Newman issued another postcard with the title printed twice, once in upper case letters and again in lower case letters, as shown on the following page. *The Ladies' Home Journal* magazine published the image, titled *His Inspiration,* on the cover of their November 1914 issue.

Dangers of the Deep (No. 772)
Copyright by Reinthal & Newman. *American Sunday Monthly* magazine published the image, titled *Vacation Days,* on the cover of their July 1914 issue.

Farewell (No. 773)
Copyright by Reinthal & Newman. *Cosmopolitan* magazine published the image on the cover of their April 1915 issue.

84 HARRISON FISHER, ILLUSTRATOR

No. 768 (number variation)
Leisure Moments

No. 768
Drifting

No. 769
Drifting
(with a German caption)

No. 769
Her Favorite "Him"

No. 768
Her Favorite "Him"
(with a German caption)

No. 770
The Third Party

No. 770
The Third Party
(with a German caption)

No. 771
Inspiration

No. 771
Inspiration
(title/printing variation)

SERIES 768-773   85

No. 772
Dangers of the Deep

No. 772
Dangers of the Deep
(with a German caption)

No. 773
Farewell

No. 773
Farewell
(with a German caption)

Number 819

Reinthal & Newman's subsidiary, The House of Art, sold the postcard, titled *Here's Happiness,* No. 819, as a single card. The postcard contains a copyright notice by Reinthal & Newman, but does not contain a copyright date. No other Harrison Fisher postcards exist within this numbering sequence. Other artists illustrated cards numbered before and after No. 819. Lester Ralph illustrated card No. 818, and Philip Boileau illustrated card No. 820. *The Ladies' Home Journal* magazine originally published the image on the cover of their October 1913 issue titled *October Bride*.

No. 819
Here's Happiness

Series 832-849 (A-C)

Series 832-849 contains eighteen postcards. Both Reinthal & Newman and the Cosmopolitan Print Department issued the cards. Postcards issued by Reinthal & Newman contain a postcard number on the back of each card. Postcards issued by the Cosmopolitan Print Department contain their imprint and a series letter A, B, or C in front of Reinthal & Newman's original postcard number. Some cards exist with the Cosmopolitan Print Department imprint covered with a thick black line, and Reinthal & Newman's name printed below. The different types of postcard backs appear in Chapter 5 titled *Postcard Backs*. The postcards were sold in sets of six with the following postcard numbers: 832-837 (Series A), 838-843 (Series B), and 844-849 (Series C).

As noted in the postcard descriptions the postcards contain a copyright notice by The Star Company (*American Sunday Monthly* magazine), or *Cosmopolitan* magazine. From 1915 to 1917, these companies originally published the postcard images on the covers of their magazine. Some of the images appear on *Nash's* magazine, a publication owned by William Randolph Hearst, owner of *Cosmopolitan* magazine, and sold in Great Britain.

Series A, 832-837

Wireless (Series A, No. 832)
Copyright by The Star Co. *American Sunday Monthly* magazine published the image on the cover of their October 1916 issue.

Neptune's Daughter (Series A, No. 833)
Copyright by Cosmopolitan Magazine. *Cosmopolitan* magazine published the image on the cover of their August 1916 issue. *Nash's* magazine published the image on the cover of their September 1916 issue.

Her Game (Series A, No. 834)
Copyright by Cosmopolitan Magazine. *Cosmopolitan* magazine published the image on the cover of their June 1916 issue. *Nash's* magazine published the image on the cover of their August 1916 issue.

All Mine (Series A, No. 835)
Copyright by Cosmopolitan Magazine. *Cosmopolitan* magazine published the image on the cover of their December 1916 issue. *Nash's* magazine published the image on the cover of their February 1917 issue.

On Summer Seas (Series A, No. 836)
Copyright by Cosmopolitan Magazine. The image appears on a Finnish postcard within the N<u>o</u>. 30/25 Series. *Cosmopolitan* magazine published the image on the cover of their July 1916 issue. *Nash's* magazine published the image on the cover of their October 1916 issue.

Autumn's Beauty (Series A, No. 837)
Copyright by Cosmopolitan Magazine. The image appears on two Finnish postcards, No. 30/25 Series and No Identification Series. *Cosmopolitan* magazine published the image on the cover of their November 1916 issue. *Nash's* magazine published the image on the cover of their January 1917 issue.

Series B, 838-843

The Only Pebble (Series B, No. 838)
Copyright by The Star Co. The image appears on a Finnish postcard within the No Identification Series. Another postcard exists with a holiday greeting overprint. *American Sunday Monthly* magazine published the image on the cover of their August 1915 issue.

A Love Score (Series B, No. 839)
Copyright by The Star Co. *American Sunday Monthly* magazine published the image on the cover of their July 1915 issue.

Spring Business (Series B, No. 840)
Copyright by The Star Co. *American Sunday Monthly* magazine published the image on the cover of their May 1916 issue.

The King of Hearts (Series B, No. 841)
Copyright by Cosmopolitan Magazine. The image appears on a Finnish postcard within the No. 30/25 Series. *Cosmopolitan* magazine published the image on the cover of their September 1916 issue. *Nash's* magazine published the image on the cover of their December 1916 issue.

Fair and Warmer (Series B, No. 842)
Copyright by The Star Co. The image appears on a Finnish postcard within the Real Photo Type Series. *American Sunday Monthly* magazine published the image on the cover of their March 1916 issue.

Baby Mine (Series B, No. 843)
Copyright by Cosmopolitan Magazine. The image appears on a Finnish postcard within the No. 30/25 Series. *Cosmopolitan* magazine published the image on the cover of their January 1916 issue. *Nash's* magazine published the image on the cover of their April 1916 issue.

Series C, 844-849

Compensation (Series C, No. 844)
Copyright by The Star Co. *American Sunday Monthly* magazine published the image on the cover of their August 1916 issue.

Sparring for Time (Series C, No. 845)
Copyright by The Star Co. *American Sunday Monthly* magazine published the image on the cover of their September 1916 issue.

Confidences (Series C, No. 846)
Copyright by The Star Co. *American Sunday Monthly* magazine published the image on the cover of their July 1916 issue.

Her Future (Series C, No. 847)
Copyright by Cosmopolitan Magazine. *Cosmopolitan* magazine published the image on the cover of their October 1916 issue. *Nash's* magazine published the image on the cover of their November 1916 issue.

Day Dreams (Series C, No. 848)
Copyright by Cosmopolitan Magazine. The image appears on two Finnish postcards, No. 30/25 Series and the Real Photo Type Series. *Cosmopolitan* magazine published the image on the cover of their May 1916 issue.

Muriel (Series C, No. 849)
Copyright by Cosmopolitan Magazine. The image appears on a Finnish postcard within the No. 30/25 Series. *Cosmopolitan* magazine published the image on the cover of their April 1916 issue. *Nash's* magazine published the image on the cover of their June 1916 issue.

HARRISON FISHER, ILLUSTRATOR

Series A, No. 832
Wireless

Series A, No. 833
Neptune's Daughter

Series A, No. 834
Her Game

Series A, No. 835
All Mine

Series A, No. 836
On Summer Seas

Series A, No. 837
Autumn's Beauty

Series B, No. 838
The Only Pebble

Series B, No. 839
A Love Score

Series B, No. 840
Spring Business

Series B, No. 841
The King of Hearts

Series B, No. 842
Fair and Warmer

Series B, No. 843
Baby Mine

SERIES 832-849   91

Series C, No. 844
Compensation

Series C, No. 845
Sparring for Time

Series C, No. 846
Confidences

Series C, No. 847
Her Future

Series C, No. 848
Day Dreams

Series C, No. 849
Muriel

Number 856

Reinthal & Newman issued and copyrighted the postcard, titled *The Song of the Soul*, No. 856. No other Harrison Fisher postcards exist within the 850 numbering sequence. The postcard does not have a copyright date, but a postcard number appears on the back of the card. The same image appears on two additional postcards within Series 108, titled *The Artist* and *Song of the Soul*. Both cards contain a copyright notice by Charles Scribner's Sons. The image also appears on a Danish postcard within the Uitg. de Muinck Series, titled *The Artist*, No. R 217, and on a Bulgarian postcard within the Apollon Sophia Series titled *La Musique (Music)*.

    The image appears in two of Fisher's art books, *American Girls in Miniature* titled *Song of the Soul*, and *Fair Americans* titled *The Artist*. The *Ladies' Home Journal* magazine published the image in their August 1910 issue as a full-page black and white illustration, titled *The Musical Girl*, and part of *The Girls I Like Best Series*.

No. 856
The Song of the Soul

Series 860-877 (D-F)

Series 860-877 contains eighteen postcards. Both Reinthal & Newman and the Cosmopolitan Print Department issued the cards. Postcards issued by Reinthal & Newman contain a postcard number on the back of each card. Postcards issued by the Cosmopolitan Print Department contain their imprint, and a series letter, D, E, or F in front of Reinthal & Newman's original postcard number. Some cards exist with the Cosmopolitan Print Department imprint covered with a thick black line, and Reinthal & Newman's name printed below. The different types of postcard backs appear in Chapter 5 titled *Postcard Backs*. The postcards were sold in sets of six with the following postcard numbers: 860-865 (Series D), 866-871 (Series E), and 872-877 (Series F).

As noted in the postcard descriptions the postcards contain a copyright notice by The Star Company (*American Sunday Monthly* magazine, *Good Housekeeping* magazine, or *Cosmopolitan* magazine. From 1915 to 1917, these companies originally published the images on the covers of their magazine. Only one postcard image, titled *I'm Ready*, did not appear on the cover of a magazine, or on any other source within Fisher's work. Some of the images appear on *Nash's* magazine, a publication owned by William Randolph Hearst, owner of *Cosmopolitan* magazine, and sold in Great Britain.

The Tin Decorating Company (Tindeco) reproduced the image, titled *Reflections*, on candy tins. Photographs of the candy tins appear in Chapter 14, titled *Candy Boxes & Tins*, within *The Complete Works of Harrison Fisher* reference book.

Series D, 860-865

By Right of Conquest (Series D, No. 860)
Copyright 1917 by Cosmopolitan Magazine. *Cosmopolitan* magazine published the image on the cover of their May 1917 issue.

The Evening Hour (Series D, No. 861)
Copyright 1917 by Cosmopolitan Magazine. *Cosmopolitan* magazine published the image on the cover of their December 1917 issue. *Nash's* published the image on the cover of their March 1918 issue.

Caught Napping (Series D, No. 862)
Copyright 1917 by Cosmopolitan Magazine. The image appears on a Finnish postcard within the No. 30/25 Series. *Cosmopolitan* magazine published the image on the cover of their September 1917 issue. *Nash's* magazine published the image on the cover of their November 1917 issue.

A Novice (Series D, No. 863)
Copyright 1917 by Cosmopolitan Magazine. The image appears on three Finnish postcards, Numbered Series N:o 7, Pain Karjalan Kirjap Series N:o 7, and the Real Photo Type Series. *Cosmopolitan* magazine published the image on the cover of their June 1917 issue. *Nash's* magazine published the image on the cover of their July 1917 issue.

Winners (Series D, No. 864)
Copyright 1917 by Cosmopolitan Magazine. The image appears on two Finnish postcards, No. 30/25 Series and the Reversed Image Series. *Cosmopolitan* magazine published the image on the cover of their April 1917 issue. *Nash's* magazine published the image on the cover of their June 1917 issue.

A Midsummer Reverie (Series D, No. 865)
Copyright 1917 by Cosmopolitan Magazine. The image appears on three Finnish postcards, No. 30/25 Series, Numbered Series N:o 10, and Pain Karjalan Kirjap Series N:o 10. *Cosmopolitan* magazine published the image on the cover of their August 1917 issue. *Nash's* magazine published the image, titled *A Summer Reverie,* on the cover of their September 1917 issue.

Series E, 866-871

When the Leaves Turn (Series E, No. 866)
Copyright 1917 by Cosmopolitan Magazine. The image appears on a Finnish postcard within the No. 30/25 Series. *Cosmopolitan* magazine published the image on the cover of their November 1917 issue. *Nash's* magazine published the image on the cover of their February 1918 issue.

Over the Teacup (Series E, No. 867)
Copyright 1917 by Cosmopolitan Magazine. *Cosmopolitan* magazine published the image on the cover of their March 1917 issue. *Nash's* magazine published the image on the cover of their April 1917 issue.

A Ripening Bud (Series E, No. 868)
Copyright 1917 by Good Housekeeping. *Good Housekeeping* magazine published the image on the cover of their July 1917 issue. *Nash's* magazine published the image on the cover of their April 1918 issue.

I'm Ready (Series E, No. 869)
Copyright 1917 by Cosmopolitan Magazine. The image does not appear on any other source within Harrison Fisher's work.

Reflections (Series E, No. 870)
Copyright 1917 by Cosmopolitan Magazine. The image appears on a Finnish postcard within the No. 30/25 Series. *Cosmopolitan* magazine published the image on the cover of their October 1917 issue. The Tin Decorating Company (Tindeco) reproduced the image on candy tins. For more information refer to Chapter 14, titled *Candy Boxes & Tins,* within *The Complete Works of Harrison Fisher* reference book.

Peggy (Series E, No. 871)
Copyright 1915 by Cosmopolitan Magazine. *Cosmopolitan* magazine published the image on the cover of their February 1915 issue. *Nash's* magazine published the image on the cover of their April 1915 issue.

Series F, 872-877

Penseroso (Series F, No. 872)
Copyright 1916 by The Star Co. *American Sunday Monthly* magazine published the image on the cover of their November 1916 issue.

The Girl He Left Behind (Series F, No. 873)
Copyright 1916 by The Star Co. *American Sunday Monthly* magazine published the image on the cover of their February 1916.

A Spring Blossom (Series F, No. 874)
Copyright 1916 by The Star Co. *American Sunday Monthly* magazine published the image on the cover of their April 1916 issue.

A Study in Contentment (Series F, No. 875)
Copyright 1917 by The Star Co. The image appears on a Finnish postcard within Reversed Image Series. *American Sunday Monthly* magazine published the image on the cover of their November 1915 issue.

A Lucky Beggar (Series F, No. 876)
Copyright 1916 by Cosmopolitan Magazine. *Cosmopolitan* and *Nash's* magazines published the image on the cover of their February 1916 issue.

Roses (Series F, No. 877)
Copyright 1915 by Cosmopolitan Magazine. *Cosmopolitan* magazine published the image on the cover of their June 1915 issue. *Nash's* magazine published the image on the cover of their July 1915 issue.

96 HARRISON FISHER, ILLUSTRATOR

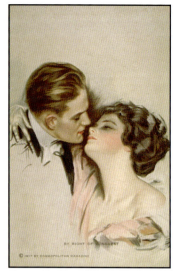
Series D, No. 860
By Right of Conquest

Series D, No. 861
The Evening Hour

Series D, No. 862
Caught Napping

Series D, No. 863
A Novice

Series D, No. 864
Winners

Series D, No. 865
A Midsummer Reverie

Series E, No. 866
When the Leaves Turn

Series E, No. 867
Over the Teacup

Series E, No. 868
A Ripening Bud

Series E, No. 869
I'm Ready

Series E, No. 870
Reflections

Series E, No. 871
Peggy

SERIES 860-877   97

Series F, No. 872
Penseroso

Series F, No. 873
The Girl He Left Behind

Series F, No. 874
A Spring Blossom

Series F, No. 875
A Study in Contentment

Series F, No. 876
A Lucky Beggar

Series F, No. 877
Roses

Series 970-979 (G-H)

Series 970-979 contains ten postcards. Both Reinthal & Newman and the Cosmopolitan Print Department issued the cards. Postcards issued by Reinthal & Newman contain a postcard number on the back of each card. Postcards issued by the Cosmopolitan Print Department contain their imprint, and a series letter, G, or H in front of Reinthal & Newman's original postcard number. Some cards exist with the Cosmopolitan Print Department imprint covered with a thick black line, and Reinthal & Newman's name printed below. The different types of postcard backs appear in Chapter 5 titled *Postcard Backs*. According to the 1919 Cosmopolitan Print Department catalog Series G originally consisted of four, special patriotic World War I, postcards numbered 976-979. Later, Cosmopolitan added additional postcard images to Series G, titled *Chums, Cynthia,* and *The Dancing Girl,* that were originally part of Series H.

As noted in the postcard descriptions the postcards contain a copyright notice by *Cosmopolitan* magazine, *International* magazine, or *Puck* magazine. In 1918, these companies originally published the images on the covers of their magazine. Some of the images appear on *Nash's* magazine, a publication owned by William Randolph Hearst, owner of *Cosmopolitan* magazine, and sold in Great Britain.

The Tin Decorating Company (Tindeco) reproduced the image, titled *The Dancing Girl,* on candy tins. Photographs of the candy tins appear in Chapter 14, titled *Candy Boxes & Tins,* within *The Complete Works of Harrison Fisher* reference book.

Series H, 970-975

Chums (Series H, No. 970)
Copyright 1918 by Cosmopolitan Magazine. Another postcard exists with Series G printed on the back of the card. *Cosmopolitan* magazine published the image on the cover of their June 1918 issue.

Cynthia (Series H, No. 971)
Copyright 1918 by International Magazine Co. Another postcard exists with Series G printed on the back of the card. *Cosmopolitan* magazine published the image on the cover of their October 1918 issue.

A Forest Flower (Series H, No. 972)
Copyright by Cosmopolitan Magazine. *Cosmopolitan* magazine published the image on the cover of their September 1918 issue. *Nash's* magazine published the image on the cover of their February 1919 issue.

The Dancing Girl (Series H, No. 973)
Copyright by Puck Magazine. Another postcard exists with Series G printed on the back of the card. *Puck* magazine published the image on the cover of their August 1918 issue. The Tin Decorating Company (Tindeco) reproduced the image on candy tins.

Each Stitch a Prayer (Series H, No. 974)
Copyright by Cosmopolitan Magazine. *Cosmopolitan* magazine published the image on the cover of their April 1918 issue. *Nash's* magazine published the image, titled *Every Stitch a Prayer,* on the cover of their July 1918 issue.

The Sailor Maid (Series H, No. 975)
Copyright by International Magazine Co. *Puck* magazine published the image on the cover of their September 1918 issue.

Series G, 976-979

My Man (Series G, No. 976)
Copyright 1918 by Cosmopolitan Magazine. The image appears on a Finnish postcard within the No. 30/25 Series. *Cosmopolitan* magazine published the image on the cover of their February 1918 issue.

My Hero (Series G, No. 977)
Copyright by Cosmopolitan Magazine. The image appears on two Finnish postcard, No. 30/25 Series and Real Photo Type Series. *Cosmopolitan* magazine published the image, titled *Her Hero,* on the cover of their July 1918 issue.

Her Heart's in the Service (Series G, No. 978)
Copyright by Cosmopolitan Magazine. *Cosmopolitan* magazine published the image on the cover of their May 1918 issue.

Somewhere in France (Series G, No. 979)
Copyright by Cosmopolitan Magazine. *Cosmopolitan* magazine published the image on the cover of their August 1918 issue.

100 HARRISON FISHER, ILLUSTRATOR

Series H, No. 970
Chums

Series H, No. 971
Cynthia

Series H, No. 972
A Forest Flower

Series H, No. 973
The Dancing Girl

Series H, No. 974
Each Stitch a Prayer

Series H, No. 975
The Sailor Maid

Series G, No. 976
My Man

Series G, No. 977
My Hero

Series G, No. 978
Her Heart's in the Service

Series G, No. 979
Somewhere in France

Series 1000 - American Reprints

The following six postcards are American Reprints. Reinthal & Newman issued the images earlier with different postcard numbers. A postcard number, No. 1000 through 1005, appears on the back of each card.

Drifting (No. 1000)
Refer to Reinthal & Newman postcard No. 768.

Cherry Ripe (No. 1001)
Refer to Reinthal & Newman postcard No. 192.

Beauties (No. 1002)
Refer to Reinthal & Newman postcard No. 196.

Vanity (No. 1003)
Refer to Reinthal & Newman postcard No. 195.

Maid to Worship (No. 1004)
Refer to Reinthal & Newman postcard No. 203.

And Yet Her Eyes Can Look Wise (No. 1005)
Refer to Reinthal & Newman postcard No. 200

No. 1000
Drifting

No. 1001
Cherry Ripe

No. 1002
Beauties

No. 1003
Vanity

No. 1004
Maid to Worship

No. 1005
And Yet Her Eyes Can Look Wise

Series 1488

Series 1488 contains a set of twelve postcards issued by Wildt & Kray—a European distributor of postcards for Reinthal & Newman. All postcards within the series contain Wildt & Kray's imprint and the series number, 1488, printed on the back of a standard Reinthal & Newman postcard. As noted in the postcard descriptions, Reinthal & Newman originally published all of the images within the Unnumbered Series, and five of the images within Series 107. Series 1488 and the Unnumbered Series are the only postcards that contain the words "Printed in U.S.A." inside the stamp box. For collectors who enjoy collecting number variations, the 1488 Series provides a challenge.

After the Dance (Series 1488)
Copyright 1907 by the Curtis Publishing Company. Reinthal & Newman published the image within the Unnumbered Series. The image appears in Fisher's art book *The Harrison Fisher Book*. *The Saturday Evening Post* magazine published the image on the cover of their February 2, 1907 issue.

American Beauties (Series 1488)
Copyright 1907 by Charles Scribner's Sons. Reinthal & Newman published the image within the Unnumbered Series and Series 107. The image appears on two Finnish postcards, Real Photo Type Series and W. & G. American Series N:o 7001/1-35. The image appears in two of Fisher's art books, *The American Girl* and *The Harrison Fisher Book*. *Success* magazine published the image as a full-page black and white illustration in their March 1908 issue.

The Critical Moment (Series 1488)
Copyright 1905 by Charles Scribner's Sons. Reinthal & Newman published the image within the Unnumbered Series. The image appears on a German postcard within the Alfred Schweizer/MEU Series. The image appears in Fisher's art book *The Harrison Fisher Book*. Reinthal & Newman sold the postcard in a frame and printed the following information on the back of the frame: "Miniatures from Life, Harrison Fisher's Society Sketches, Hand Colored, Series No. 727."

A Fair Driver (Series 1488)
Copyright 1907 by P.F. Collier & Son. Reinthal & Newman published the image within the Unnumbered Series and Series 107. The image appears in two of Fisher's art books, *The American Girl* and *Fair Americans*. The image appears in the art book, *Thirty Favorite Paintings,* titled *How Pleasant It Is to Have Money*. *Collier's* magazine published the image, titled *The Little Heiress,* on the cover of their November 2, 1907 issues. Charles Scribner's Sons published the image in their 1909 Harrison Fisher art calendar.

The Motor Girl (Series 1488)
Copyright 1908 by Charles Scribner's Sons. Reinthal & Newman published the image within the Unnumbered Series. The image appears in two of Fisher's art books, *The American Girl* and *Fair Americans*. The image appears in the art book, *Thirty Favorite Paintings,* titled *Ready for a Spin*. *Collier's* magazine published the image, titled *Ready for the Road,* on the cover of their May 9, 1908 issue. Charles Scribner's Sons published the image in their 1909 Harrison Fisher art calendar.

Over the Teacup (Series 1488)
Copyright 1907 by Charles Scribner's Sons. Reinthal & Newman published the image within the Unnumbered Series and Series 107. The image appears in two of Fisher's art books, *The American Girl* and *The Harrison Fisher Book*.

Ready for the Run (Series 1488)
Copyright 1907 by Charles Scribner's Sons. Reinthal & Newman published the image within the Unnumbered Series. The image appears in Fisher's art book *The Harrison Fisher Book*.

Ruth (Series 1488)
Copyright 1907 by the Curtis Publishing Company. Reinthal & Newman published the image within the Unnumbered Series. In 1907, Dodd, Mead published the image on a book advertising postcard to promote the sales of a novel, *The Stooping Lady,* written by Maurice Henry Hewlett. A.L. Burt reprinted the novel. The image of *Ruth* appears on the frontispiece of both editions. The image appears in Fisher's art book *The Harrison Fisher Book*. *The Saturday Evening Post* magazine published the image on the cover of their January 12, 1907 issue.

A Tennis Champion (Series 1488)
Copyright 1907 by the Curtis Publishing Company. Reinthal & Newman published the image within the Unnumbered Series. The image appears in two of Fisher's art books, *The American Girl* titled *A Tennis Champion,* and *The Harrison Fisher Book* titled *The Champion*. *The Saturday Evening Post* magazine published the image on the cover of their May 25, 1907 issue.

A Thoroughbred (Series 1488)
Copyright 1907 by Charles Scribner's Sons. Reinthal & Newman published the image within the Unnumbered Series and Series 107. The image appears on two Danish postcards, Uitgave Louis Diefenthal Series and Uitg. de Muinck Series No. R 193.. The image appears in two of Fisher's art books, *The American Girl* titled *A Thoroughbred*, and *The Harrison Fisher Book* titled *A Blue-Ribbon Winner*. *The Saturday Evening Post* magazine published the image on the cover of their April 13, 1907 issue.

Those Bewitching Eyes (Series 1488)
Copyright 1906 by Charles Scribner's Sons. Reinthal & Newman published the image within the Unnumbered Series and Series 107. The image appears on two Russian postcards, Rishar Series No. 117 and Linen Series No. 6. The image appears in two of Fisher's art books, *The American Girl* and *The Harrison Fisher Book*. The image appears on the book cover inlay for the art book titled *Pictures in Color by Famous American Artists*. *The Ladies' Home Journal* magazine published the image on the cover of their October 1907 issue.

The Winter Girl (Series 1488)
Copyright 1907 by Charles Scribner's Sons. Reinthal & Newman published the image within the Unnumbered Series. The image appears in Fisher's art book *The Harrison Fisher Book*. *The Saturday Evening Post* magazine published the image on the cover of their March 30, 1907 issue.

SERIES 1488 105

Series 1488
After the Dance

Series 1488
American Beauties

Series 1488
The Critical Moment

Series 1488
A Fair Driver

Series 1488
The Motor Girl

Series 1488
Over the Teacup

Series 1488
Ready for the Run

Series 1488
Ruth

Series 1488
A Tennis Champion

Series 1488
A Thoroughbred

Series 1488
Those Bewitching Eyes

Series 1488
The Winter Girl

Series 2000 - English Reprints

The following thirty-four postcards are English Reprints. Reinthal & Newman issued all of the cards, except for one, titled *What to See in America,* No. 2054, in earlier series with different postcard numbers.

Two images, *Preparing to Conquer* No. 2051 and *The Kiss* No. 2053, are image variations of the postcards issued earlier by Reinthal & Newman. Three images, *Fair Exhibitor* No. 2041, *Serenade* No. 2043, and *Good Little Indian* No. 2047 contain title variations. The original titles are *A Fair Exhibitor, The Serenade,* and *Girlie.* Two images, *Undecided* No. 2044 and *Contentment* No. 2050, appeared earlier within a water color series on an absorbent buff-colored card stock. Reinthal & Newman issued the English Reprints on regular card stock.

Love Lyrics (No. 2040)
Refer to Reinthal & Newman postcard No. 257.

Fair Exhibitor (No. 2041)
Refer to Reinthal & Newman postcard No. 610 titled *A Fair Exhibitor.*

Can't You Speak? (No. 2042)
Refer to Reinthal & Newman postcard No. 412.

Serenade (No. 2043)
Refer to Reinthal & Newman postcard No. 606 titled *The Serenade.* Another English Reprint postcard, No. 2043, exists with a German Happy New Year overprint.

Undecided (No. 2044)
Refer to Reinthal & Newman Water Color Series postcard No. 389.

Behave! (No. 2045)
Refer to Reinthal & Newman postcard No. 302.

Princess Pat (No. 2046)
Refer to Reinthal & Newman postcard No. 407.

Good Little Indian (No. 2047)
Refer to Reinthal & Newman postcard No. 261 titled *Girlie.*

Chocolate (No. 2048)
Refer to Reinthal & Newman postcard No. 617.

Beauty and Value (No. 2049)
Refer to Reinthal & Newman postcard No. 262.

Contentment (No. 2050)
Refer to Reinthal & Newman Water Color Series postcard No. 383.

Preparing to Conquer (No. 2051)
Refer to Reinthal & Newman postcard No. 256 (image variation).

The Kiss (No. 2053)
Refer to Reinthal & Newman Series 108 (image variation).

What to See in America (No. 2054)
The image was not issued on another postcard. The image appears in Fisher's art book *Harrison Fisher Girls*.

Paddling Their Own Canoe (No. 2069)
Refer to Reinthal & Newman postcard No. 611.

Good Morning, Mamma (No. 2076)
Refer to Reinthal & Newman postcard No. 608

The Pink of Perfection (No. 2086)
Refer to Reinthal & Newman postcard No. 404.

He Won't Bite- (No. 2087)
Refer to Reinthal & Newman postcard No. 405.

Following the Race (No. 2088)
Refer to Reinthal & Newman postcard No. 184.

The Rose (No. 2089)
Refer to Reinthal & Newman postcard No. 181.

Well Protected (No. 2090)
Refer to Reinthal & Newman postcard No. 180.

Sketching (No. 2091)
Refer to Reinthal & Newman postcard No. 616.

Ready and Waiting (No. 2092)
Refer to Reinthal & Newman postcard No. 418.

The Parasol (No. 2093)
Refer to Reinthal & Newman postcard No. 419.

Courting Attention (No. 2094)
Refer to Reinthal & Newman postcard No. 422.

Mary (No. 2095)
Refer to Reinthal & Newman postcard No. 421.

Refreshments (No. 2096)
Refer to Reinthal & Newman postcard No. 406.

Isn't He Sweet? (No. 2097)
Refer to Reinthal & Newman postcard No. 409.

The Old Miniature (No. 2098)
Refer to Reinthal & Newman Series 101.

Beauties (No. 2099)
Refer to Reinthal & Newman Series 101.

Odd Moments (No. 2100)
Refer to Reinthal & Newman Series 101.

Tea Time (No. 2101)
Refer to Reinthal & Newman postcard No. 612.

Good Night! (No. 2102)
Refer to Reinthal & Newman postcard No. 259.

A Prairie Belle (No. 2103)
Refer to Reinthal & Newman postcard No. 263.

SERIES 2000 - ENGLISH REPRINTS 109

No. 2040
Love Lyrics

No. 2041
Fair Exhibitor

No. 2042
Can't You Speak?

No. 2043
Serenade

No. 2043
Serenade
(with overprint)

No. 2044
Undecided

No. 2045
Behave!

No. 2046
Princess Pat

No. 2047
Good Little Indian

No. 2048
Chocolate

No. 2049
Beauty and Value

No. 2050
Contentment

HARRISON FISHER, ILLUSTRATOR

No. 2051
Preparing to Conquer

No. 2053
The Kiss

No. 2054
What to See in America

No. 2069
Paddling Their Own Canoe

No. 2076
Good Morning, Mamma

No. 2086
The Pink of Perfection

No. 2087
He Won't Bite-

No. 2088
Following the Race

No. 2089
The Rose

No. 2090
Well Protected

No. 2091
Sketching

No. 2092
Ready and Waiting

SERIES 2000 - ENGLISH REPRINTS   111

No. 2093
The Parasol

No. 2094
Courting Attention

No. 2095
Mary

No. 2096
Refreshments

No. 2097
Isn't He Sweet?

No. 2098
The Old Miniature

No. 2099
Beauties

No. 2100
Odd Moments

No. 2101
Tea Time

No. 2102
Good Night!

No. 2103
A Prairie Belle

CHAPTER TWO

European Postcards

Austrian - B.K.W.I.

B.K.W.I. distributed *Naughty, Naughty!*–the only Harrison Fisher postcard, issued in Austria, known to exist. The postcard contains the initials B.K.W.I. printed on the back of the card. The card is hand-tinted on an absorbent buff-colored card stock similar to the card stock used in the Reinthal & Newman Water Color Series. Due to the time consuming, labor oriented process of tinting cards by hand, publishers did not produce them in the same quantities as other cards. As a result this postcard is extremely difficult to locate.

Reinthal & Newman issued the image on postcard No. 185, titled *Naughty, Naughty!,* shown on page 51, where the image receives it's name. In 1912, Charles Scribner's Sons published the image in Fisher's art book *American Girls in Miniature*. In 1911 and 1913, Charles Scribner's Sons published a variation of the image, titled *Rejected,* in *Fair Americans* and *A Girls Life and Other Pictures*. *Cosmopolitan* magazine originally published the image on the cover of their May 1911 issue as shown below.

B.K.W.I. (Naughty, Naughty!)

May 1911 Cosmopolitan Magazine

Bulgarian - Apollon Sophia

Apollon Sophia distributed *La Musique (Music)*–the only Harrison Fisher postcard known to exist from The Balkan States, Bulgaria. The image also appears on a Danish postcard within the Uitg. de Muinck Series, titled *The Artist,* No. R 217. Reinthal & Newman issued the image on three postcards, Series 108 titled *The Artist,* Series 108 titled *Song of the Soul,* and No. 856 titled *The Song of the Soul.*

    The Ladies' Home Journal magazine originally published the image as a full-page black and white illustration, and part of *The Girls I Like Best Series,* titled *The Musical Girl,* within their August 1910 issue. For more information regarding the series refer to Chapter 7, titled *Series,* within *The Complete Works of Harrison Fisher* reference book. In 1911, Charles Scribner's Sons published the image in Fisher's art book, *Fair Americans,* titled *The Artist.* In 1912, Charles Scribner's Sons reprinted the image in Fisher's art book, *American Girls in Miniature,* titled *Song of the Soul.*

Apollon Sophia
La Musique (Music)

Danish - Uitg. de Muinck Series

Thirteen Fisher images have surfaced within the Uitg. de Muinck Series. It is believed that at least two additional postcards, possibly more, exist with the following images: *The Trousseau* and *The Wedding*. Uitg. de Muinck & Co. located in Amsterdam, The Netherlands, issued the postcards on an absorbent buff-colored card stock. The publisher issued a postcard number on the back of each card with the letter R in front of the number. The publisher issued *The Kiss* with an image variation, and the letter R printed after the number. This image variation appears on page 118.

The Kiss (R 185) (186 R)
Published by Uitg. de Muinck. The image appears on another postcard No. 186 R with the title printed in a different location on the front of the card. The image appears on three Russian postcards, Modern Art Sofia Series, Sepia Series, and E.K. Series. The image appears on a Reinthal & Newman postcard No. 2053. The image appears in two of Fisher's art books *Fair Americans* and *A Girls Life and Other Pictures*. Reinthal & Newman issued a postcard image variation, short view, within Series 108. The same image variation appears in Fisher's art book *The Little Gift Book*. *The Ladies' Home Journal* magazine published another image variation, long view, on the cover of their July 1910 issue. Reinthal & Newman sold the postcard in a frame with a poem underneath the image.

Dumb Luck (R 188)
Published by Uitg. de Muinck. The image appears on a Reinthal & Newman postcard within Series 108. The image appears in two of Fisher's art books, *The American Girl* and *Fair Americans*. *The Saturday Evening Post* magazine published the image on the cover of their November 28, 1908 issue.

Danger (R 191)
Published by Uitg. de Muinck. The image appears on a Reinthal & Newman postcard within Series 101. Reinthal & Newman sold the postcard in a frame with a poem underneath the image. The image appears in two of Fisher's art books, *American Girls in Miniature* and *Fair Americans*. *Cosmopolitan* magazine published the image on the cover of their May 1909 issue.

A Study Hour (R 192)
Published by Uitg. de Muinck. The image appears on a Reinthal & Newman postcard within Series 101 titled *The Study Hour*. The image appears in two of Fisher's art books, *The American Girl* and *Fair Americans*. *The Ladies' Home Journal* magazine published the image as a black & white illustration, titled *The College Girl at Her Studies,* within their April 1908 issue.

Thoroughbred (R 193)
Published by Uitg. de Muinck. The image appears on another Danish postcard published by Uitgave Louis Diefenthal. The image appears on two Reinthal & Newman postcards, Unnumbered Series and Series 101. The image appears in two of Fisher's art books, *The American Girl* titled *A Thoroughbred* and *The Harrison Fisher Book* titled *A Blue-Ribbon Winner*. *The Saturday Evening Post* magazine published the image on the cover of their April 13, 1907 issue.

The Ambush (R 197)
Published by Uitg. de Muinck. The image appears on a Reinthal & Newman postcard within Series 108. The image appears in two of Fisher's art books, *Fair Americans* and *Pictures in Color*. *The Ladies' Home Journal* magazine published the image, as a color illustration, within their September 1909 issue.

The Artist (R 217)   Not shown
Published by Uitg. de Muinck. The image appears on a Bulgarian postcard titled *La Musique (Music)*. The image appears on three Reinthal & Newman postcards, Series 108 titled *The Artist*, Series 108 titled *Song of the Soul*, and No. 856 titled *The Song of the Soul*. The image appears in two of Fisher's art books, *American Girls in Miniature* and *Fair Americans*. *The Ladies' Home Journal* magazine published the image as a black and white illustration, titled *The Musical Girl*, within their August 1910 issue.

The Proposal   (R 223)
Published by Uitg. de Muinck. The image appears on two Reinthal & Newman postcards, No. 186 and No. 468. The image appears in two of Fisher's art books, *American Girls in Miniature* and *A Girl's Life and Other Pictures*. *The Ladies' Home Journal* magazine published the image as a black and white illustration, titled *The Supreme Moment-The Proposal*, within their March 15, 1911 issue.

The Honeymoon   (R 224)
Published by Uitg. de Muinck. The image appears on two Reinthal & Newman postcards, No. 189 and No. 471. The image appears in two of Fisher's art books, *American Girls in Miniature* and *A Girl's Life and Other Pictures*. *The Ladies' Home Journal* magazine published the image as a black and white illustration, titled *The Honeymoon Abroad*, within their July 1911 issue.

The First Evening in Their Own Home (R 225)
Published by Uitg. de Muinck. The image appears on two Reinthal & Newman postcards, No. 190 and No. 472. The image appears in two of Fisher's art books, *American Girls in Miniature* and *A Girl's Life and Other Pictures*. *The Ladies' Home Journal* magazine published the image as a black and white illustration within their August 1911 issue.

Their New Love (R 226)
Published by Uitg. de Muinck. The image appears on two Reinthal & Newman postcards, No. 191 and No. 473. The image appears in two of Fisher's art books, *American Girls in Miniature* and *A Girl's Life and Other Pictures*. *The Ladies' Home Journal* magazine published the image on the cover of their October 1911 issue. R&N sold the image on a print, mounted in a frame, with a poem titled *Mother*.

A Modern Eve (R 231)
Published by Uitg. de Muinck. The image appears on a Reinthal & Newman postcard within Series 123. The image appears in two of Fisher's art books, *The Harrison Fisher Book* and *Pictures in Color*.

Lost? (R 232)
Published by Uitg. de Muinck. The image appears on a Reinthal & Newman postcard within Series 108. The image appears in two of Fisher's art books, *Fair Americans* and *Pictures in Color*.

You Will Marry a Dark Man   (R 233)
Published by Uitg. de Muinck. The image appears on a Reinthal & Newman postcard within Series 123. The image appears in two of Fisher's art books, *The Harrison Fisher Book* and *Pictures in Color*.

Uitg. de Muinck No. R 185
The Kiss

Uitg. de Muinck No. 186 R
The Kiss (variation)

Uitg. de Muinck No. R 188
Dumb Luck

Uitg. de Muinck No. R 191
Danger

Uitg. de Muinck No. R 192
A Study Hour

Uitg. de Muinck No. R 193
Thoroughbred

Uitg. de Muinck No. R 197
The Ambush

Uitg. de Muinck No. R 223
The Proposal

Uitg. de Muinck No. R 224
The Honeymoon

Uitg. de Muinck No. R 225
The First Evening in Their Own Home

Uitg. de Muinck No. R 226
Their New Love

Uitg. de Muinck No. R 231
A Modern Eve

Uitg. de Muinck No. R 232
Lost?

Uitg. de Muinck No. R 233
You Will Marry a Dark Man

Danish - Uitg. L. Diefenthal 300 Series

One Fisher image has surfaced within the Uitg. L. Diefenthal 300 Series. The publisher issued the postcard with the number, 366, printed on the back of the card. The author believes that five additional postcards exist within the series with the following images: *The Dollarprincess in Japan, England, Ireland, Italy,* and *France.* One postcard shown below is hand-tinted on an absorbent buff-colored card stock. The publisher also issued the image in black and white with the same postcard number as shown below.

In 1909, *The Ladies' Home Journal* magazine originally published the series, titled *American Girls Abroad,* as full-page black and white illustrations within their magazine. From 1910 to 1912, Charles Scribner's Sons published the series in three of Fisher's art books, *American Girls in Miniature, Fair Americans,* and *Pictures in Color.* Reinthal & Newman issued the images as a set of six postcards within Series 102.

Uitg. L. Diefenthal No. 366, Hand-Tinted
The Dollarprincess in Holland

Uitg. L. Diefenthal No. 366, Black and White
The Dollarprincess in Holland

Danish - Uitgave Louis Diefenthal Sepia Series

One Fisher image has surfaced within the Uitgave Louis Diefenthal Sepia Series. The author believes that additional postcards exist within the series that have not surfaced yet. The publisher issued the postcard with a title, but without a postcard number.

The image appears on another Danish postcard within the Uitg. de Muinck Series No. R 193, shown on page 118. The image appears on two Reinthal & Newman postcards, Unnumbered Series and Series 101. *The Saturday Evening Post* magazine originally published the image on the cover of their April 13, 1907 issue. In 1907 and 1909, Charles Scribner's Sons reprinted the image in two of Fisher's art books, *The American Girl* titled *A Thoroughbred* and *The Harrison Fisher Book* titled *A Blue-Ribbon Winner*.

Uitgave Louis Diefenthal Sepia Series
A Thoroughbred

Finnish - No 30/25 Series

The No 30/25 Series is a favorite among Harrison Fisher collectors. It represents the largest Finnish series illustrated by Fisher. The series of twenty-five postcards provides a challenge to complete the entire set. Very few complete sets exist. The numbering system used for the series, No 30/25, appears on the back of each postcard. The publisher used the first number "30" to identify progressive postcard sets. The second number "25" identifies the number of postcards within the set. The postcards do not have any other source of identification. Based on the numbering system, research indicates that Juusela and Levanen, located in Helsinki, Finland, published the series.

The postcards do not contain titles. Twenty of the images, within the series, appear on Reinthal & Newman postcards where the images receive their names. The other five images appear on prints sold by The Cosmopolitan Print Department where the images receive their names. Collectors will find both signed and unsigned cards. Unsigned cards are more difficult to locate, and usually demand slightly higher values. The publisher may have printed the cards twice, once with Fisher's signature and once without, or the difference may have occurred for another reason. The publisher printed the postcards on two different types of card stock, textured and smooth. The majority of cards found today appear on a textured card stock. A few postcards exist with a holiday greeting overprint. Publishers added overprints to increase postcard sales during major holidays such as Easter, Christmas, and New Years. They printed them in a variety of languages, English, Dutch, Finnish, German, and Swedish. Postcards with overprints have become extremely difficult to locate, and increase the value of the card. As noted in the postcard descriptions, all of the images originally appeared on magazine covers for *Cosmopolitan, Nash's,* or *The Saturday Evening Post* from 1911 to 1918. The Tin Decorating Company (Tindeco) reprinted two images, *Reflections* and *The Snow Bird,* on candy tins. Photographs of the candy tins appear in Chapter 14, titled *Candy Boxes & Tins,* within *The Complete Works of Harrison Fisher* reference book.

All Mine! (No 30/25)
Published by Juusela and Levanen. The image appears on a Reinthal & Newman postcard No. 303. *Cosmopolitan* magazine published the image on the cover of their September 1912 issue. The image appears in Fisher's art book *The Little Gift Book*. The Cosmopolitan Print Department sold the image on a print titled *Sonny Boy*.

An Idle Hour (No 30/25)
Published by Juusela and Levanen. The image does not appear on a Reinthal & Newman postcard. *Cosmopolitan* magazine published the image on the cover of their August 1914 issue. The Cosmopolitan Print Dept. sold the image on a print, titled *An Idle Hour,* where the image receives its name.

Autumn's Beauty (No 30/25)
Published by Juusela and Levanen. The image appears on another Finnish postcard within the No Identification Series. The image appears on a Reinthal & Newman postcard No. 837. *Cosmopolitan* magazine published the image on the cover of their November 1916 issue. *Nash's* magazine published the image on the cover of their January 1917 issue.

Baby Mine (No 30/25)
Published by Juusela and Levanen. The image appears on a Reinthal & Newman postcard No. 843. *Cosmopolitan* magazine published the image on the cover of their January 1916 issue. *Nash's* magazine published the image on the cover of their April 1916 issue.

Beauty and Value (No 30/25)
Published by Juusela and Levanen. The image appears on two Reinthal & Newman postcards, No. 262 and No. 2049. The image appears in two of Fisher's art books, *Beauties* and *The Little Gift Book*, titled *The College Girl*. *The Saturday Evening Post* magazine published the image on the cover of their June 29, 1912 issue.

Caught Napping (No 30/25)
Published by Juusela and Levanen. The image appears on a Reinthal & Newman postcard No. 862. *Cosmopolitan* magazine published the image on the cover of their September 1917 issue. *Nash's* magazine published the image on the cover of their November 1917 issue.

Close to Shore (No 30/25)
Published by Juusela and Levanen. The image appears on three other Finnish postcards, Numbered Series N:o 4, Pain. Karjalan Kirjap Series N:o 4, and Otto Andersin Series. The image appears on a Reinthal & Newman postcard No. 764. *Cosmopolitan* and *Nash's* magazine published the image on the cover of their August 1915 issue titled *A Fair Breeze*.

Day Dreams (No 30/25)
Published by Juusela and Levanen. The image appears on another Finnish postcard within the Real Photo Type Series. The image appears on a Reinthal & Newman postcard No. 848. *Cosmopolitan* magazine published the image on the cover of their May 1916 issue.

The Debutante (No 30/25)
Published by Juusela and Levanen. The image does not appear on a Reinthal & Newman postcard. *Cosmopolitan* magazine published the image on the cover of their January 1917 issue. The Cosmopolitan Print Dept. sold the image on a print, titled *The Debutante,* where the image receives its name. *Nash's* magazine published the image on the cover of their December 1917 issued titled *The Debutante.*

The King of Hearts (No 30/25)
Published by Juusela and Levanen. The image appears on a Reinthal & Newman postcard No. 841. *Cosmopolitan* magazine published the image on the cover of their September 1916 issue. *Nash's* magazine published the image on the cover of their December 1916 issue.

Love Lyrics (N͟o 30/25)
Published by Juusela and Levanen. The image appears on another Finnish postcard within the Titled Series. The image appears on a Russian postcard within the English Back Series. The image appears on two Reinthal & Newman postcards, No. 257 and No. 2040. The image appears in two of Fisher's art books, *The Little Gift Book* and *Maidens Fair*. *The Saturday Evening Post* magazine published the image on the cover of their August 5, 1911 issue.

A Midsummer Reverie (N͟o 30/25)
Published by Juusela and Levanen. The image appears on two other Finnish postcards, Numbered Series N:o 10 and Pain. Karjalan Kirjap Series N:o 10. The image appears on a Reinthal & Newman postcard No. 865. *Cosmopolitan* magazine published the image on the cover of their August 1917 issue. *Nash's* magazine published the image on the cover of their September 1917 issue titled *A Summer Reverie.*

Muriel (N͟o 30/25)
Published by Juusela and Levanen. The image appears on a Reinthal & Newman postcard No. 849. *Cosmopolitan* magazine published the image on the cover of their April 1916 issue. *Nash's* magazine published the image on the cover of their June 1916 issue.

My Hero (N͟o 30/25)
Published by Juusela and Levanen. The image appears on a Finnish postcard within the Real Photo Type Series. The image appears on a Reinthal & Newman postcard No. 977. *Cosmopolitan* magazine published the image on the cover of their July 1918 issue titled *Her Hero.*

My Man (N͟o30/25)
Published by Juusela and Levanen. The image appears on a Reinthal & Newman postcard No. 976. *Cosmopolitan* magazine published the image on the cover of their February 1918 issue.

Not Yet-But Soon (N͟o 30/25)
Published by Juusela and Levanen. The image appears on a Reinthal & Newman Water Color Series postcard No. 384. Reinthal & Newman used the postcard as part of the *Smiles and Kisses* postcard panel. *Cosmopolitan* magazine published the image on the cover of their January 1913 issue. The Cosmopolitan Print Department sold the image on a print titled *Impending*.

On Summer Seas (N͟o 30/25)
Published by Juusela and Levanen. The image appears on a Reinthal & Newman postcard No. 836. *Cosmopolitan* magazine published the image on the cover of their July 1916 issue. *Nash's* magazine published the image on the cover of their October 1916 issue.

Reflections (N͟o 30/25)
Published by Juusela and Levanen. The image appears on a Reinthal & Newman postcard No. 870. *Cosmopolitan* magazine published the image on the cover of their October 1917 issue. The Tin Decorating Company (Tindeco) reproduced the image on candy tins.

The Snow Bird (No 30/25)
Published by Juusela and Levanen. The image does not appear on a Reinthal & Newman postcard. An image variation exists on another No 30/25 postcard that contains small etched boxes in both the top corners of the card as shown on the following page. The image appears on another Finnish postcard within the Reversed Image Series. *Cosmopolitan* magazine published the image on the cover of their January 1918 issue, titled *The Snow Bird,* where the image receives its name. *Nash's* magazine published the image on the cover of their December 1918 issue. The Cosmopolitan Print Department sold the image on a print titled *The Snow Bird.* The Tin Decorating Company (Tindeco) reproduced the image on candy tins.

Stringing Them (No 30/25)
Published by Juusela and Levanen. The image does not appear on a Reinthal & Newman postcard. The publisher issued another postcard with a Finnish holiday greeting overprint. *Cosmopolitan* magazine published the image on the cover of their December 1914 issue. *Nash's* magazine published the image on the cover of their January 1916 issue.   The Cosmopolitan Print Department sold the image on a print, titled *Stringing Them,* where the image receives its name.

Two Roses (No 30/25)
Published by Juusela and Levanen. The image appears on a Reinthal & Newman Water Color Series postcard No. 382. *Cosmopolitan* magazine published the image on the cover of their August 1913 issue. *Nash's* magazine published the image on the cover of their September 1913 issue.

Welcome Home! (No 30/25)
Published by Juusela and Levanen. An image variation, with a man, appears on another Finnish postcard within the Numbered Series N:o 13. The same image variation appears on a Reinthal & Newman Water Color Series postcard No. 387. Reinthal & Newman used the postcard as part of the *Smiles and Kisses* postcard panel. *Cosmopolitan* magazine published the image on the cover of their April 1913 issue. The image appears in Fisher's art book *Beauties.*

When the Leaves Turn (No 30/25)
Published by Juusela and Levanen. The image appears on a Reinthal & Newman postcard No. 866. *Cosmopolitan* magazine published the image on the cover of their November 1917 issue. *Nash's* magazine published the image on the cover of their February 1918 issue.

Winifred (No 30/25)
Published by Juusela and Levanen. The image does not appear on a Reinthal & Newman postcard. *Cosmopolitan* magazine published the image on the cover of their October 1912 issue. The Cosmopolitan Print Department sold the image on a print, titled *Winifred,* where the image receives its name.   The image appears on the book cover inlay of Fisher's art book *A Girls Life and Other Pictures.*

Winners (No 30/25)
Published by Juusela and Levanen. The image appears on another Finnish postcard within the Reversed Image Series. The image appears on a Reinthal & Newman postcard No. 864. *Cosmopolitan* magazine published the image on the cover of their April 1917 issue. *Nash's* magazine published the image on the cover of their June 1917 issue.

126 HARRISON FISHER, ILLUSTRATOR

No 30/25 Series
(All Mine!)

No 30/25 Series
(An Idle Hour)

No 30/25 Series
(Autumn's Beauty)

No 30/25 Series
(Baby Mine)

No 30/25 Series
(Beauty and Value)

No 30/25 Series
(Caught Napping)

No 30/25 Series
(Close to Shore)

No 30/25 Series
(Day Dreams)

No 30/25 Series
(The Debutante)

No 30/25 Series
(The King of Hearts)

No 30/25 Series
(Love Lyrics)

No 30/25 Series
(A Midsummer Reverie)

FINNISH - NO 30/25 SERIES   127

No 30/25 Series
(Muriel)

No 30/25 Series
(My Hero)

No 30/25 Series
(My Man)

No 30/25 Series
(Not Yet-But Soon)

No 30/25 Series
(On Summer Seas)

No 30/25 Series
(Reflections)

No 30/25 Series
(The Snow Bird)

No 30/25 Series
(The Snow Bird) Variation with etched boxes on top corners

No 30/25 Series
(Stringing Them)

No 30/25 Series
(Stringing Them)
with overprint

No 30/25 Series
(Two Roses)

No 30/25 Series
(Welcome Home!)

No 30/25 Series
(When the Leaves Turn)

No 30/25 Series
(Winifred)

No 30/25 Series
(Winners)

Finnish - Reversed Image Series

The Reversed Image Series contains three postcards published by S & K located in Kouvola, Finland. These postcards are extremely rare, and difficult to find. It is possible that other images exist that have not surfaced yet.

The postcards are reversed images. They face the opposite direction from their original published source–on magazine covers for the *American Sunday Monthly* and *Cosmopolitan* published in 1915 through 1918. The publisher issued the postcards with a circle on the back top portion of the card with the words "S & K Kouvola" printed inside the circle, but the author has seen the image, titled *Winners,* without this identification. The postcards do not contain titles. Two of the images, *A Study in Contentment* and *Winners,* appear on Reinthal & Newman postcards where the images receive their names. *The Snow Bird* appears on the cover of *Cosmopolitan* magazine where it receives it's name.

The Tin Decorating Company (Tindeco) reproduced the image, titled *The Snow Bird,* on candy tins. Photographs of the candy tins appear in Chapter 14, titled *Candy Boxes & Tins,* within *The Complete Works of Harrison Fisher* reference book.

The Snow Bird (Reversed Image Series)
Published by S & K. The image appears on another Finnish postcard within the No 30/25 Series. The image does not appear on a Reinthal & Newman postcard. *Cosmopolitan* magazine published the image on the cover of their January 1918 issue titled, *The Snow Bird,* where the image receives its name. *Nash's* magazine published the image on the cover of their December 1918 issue. The Cosmopolitan Print Department sold the image on a print titled *The Snow Bird.* The Tin Decorating Company (Tindeco) reproduced the image on candy tins.

A Study in Contentment (Reversed Image Series)
Published by S & K. The image appears on a Reinthal & Newman postcard No. 875. The *American Sunday Monthly* magazine published the image on the cover of their November 1915 issue.

Winners (Reversed Image Series)
Published by S & K. The image appears on another Finnish postcard within the No 30/25 Series. The image appears on a Reinthal & Newman postcard No. 864. *Cosmopolitan* magazine published the image on the cover of their April 1917 issue. *Nash's* magazine published the image on the cover of their June 1917 issue.

Reversed Image Series
(The Snow Bird)

Reversed Image Series
(A Study in Contentment)

Reversed Image Series
(Winners)

Finnish - Otto Andersin Series

The Otto Andersin Series contains three postcards published by Otto Andersin located in Pori, Finland. The postcards are unique in that Otto Andersin reduced the images to 1 3/4" x 2 3/4" on a standard size postcard. No other American or European Harrison Fisher postcard contains this design. The postcards are extremely rare, and difficult to find. Due to their rarity, cards in any reasonable condition are worth adding to one's collection. The postcards do not contain titles. The images appear on Reinthal & Newman postcards where the images receive their names.

All's Well (Otto Andersin Series) Not shown
Published by Otto Andersin. The image appears on a Finnish postcard within the Real Photo Type Series. The image appears on a Reinthal & Newman Water Color Series postcard No. 381. *Cosmopolitan* magazine published the image on the cover of their September 1913 issue. *Nash's* magazine published the image on the cover of their October 1913 issue. The Tin Decorating Company (Tindeco) reproduced an image variation, titled *The Yachting Girl,* on candy tins.

Close to Shore (Otto Andersin Series)
Published by Otto Andersin. The image appears on three other Finnish postcards, Series N̲o̲ 30/25, Numbered Series N:o 4, and Pain. Karjalan Kirjap Series N:o 4. The image appears on a Reinthal & Newman postcard No. 764. *Cosmopolitan* magazine published the image on the cover of their August 1915 issue titled *A Fair Breeze.*

Drifting (Otto Andersin Series) Not shown
Published by Otto Andersin. The image appears on another Finnish postcard within the Real Photo Type Series. The image appears on two Reinthal & Newman postcards, No. 768 and No. 1000. The *American Sunday Monthly* magazine published the image on the cover of their June 1914 issue.

Otto Andersin Series
(Close to Shore)

Finnish - K.K. Oy. No 1/20 Series

The K.K. Oy. N:o 1/20 Series contains two postcard images published by Pain. Karjalan Kirjap located in Viipuri, Finland. The series has two different types of postcard backs. One back has "K.K. Oy. No 1/20-K.F.P-n kp. oy." printed on the back of the card, and the other has "KYK-KFP" printed in a circle on the back of the card. These identifications refer to the Pain. Karjalan Kirjap publisher.

The postcards do not contain titles. The image, titled *Thoroughbreds*, appears on a Reinthal & Newman postcard where the image receives it's name. The image, *Mistletoe*, received it's title from Joseph Lee Mashburn, the author of *The Super Rare Postcards of Harrison Fisher* reference book, until the actual title is identified.

Mistletoe appears on an extremely rare novelty postcard, shown on the following page, which contains a unique variation never before seen on another Harrison Fisher postcard. The card has the addition of real hair applied to the ladies head with a red satin bow. Postcard manufacturers issued a wide variety of novelty cards in an attempt to increase sales, and to outwit their primary competitors. Publishers attached all sorts of items to the face of the cards. The most frequently encountered items include real hair, feathers, beads, and pieces of cloth. The publisher applied these items by hand after printing the card. In 1912, both images originally appeared on magazine covers for *The Saturday Evening Post*.

Mistletoe (K.K. Oy. No 1/20 Series)
Published by Pain. Karjalan Kirjap. The image appears on novelty postcard with the edition of real hair and a red satin bow. The image does not appear on a Reinthal & Newman postcard. *The Saturday Evening Post* magazine published the image on the cover of their December 14, 1912 issue. Joseph Lee Mashburn titled the image.

Thoroughbreds (K.K. Oy. No 1/20 Series)
Published by Pain. Karjalan Kirjap. The image appears on a Reinthal & Newman postcard No. 304. The image appears in two of Fisher's art books, *The Little Gift Book* and *Maidens Fair*. *The Saturday Evening Post* magazine published the image on the cover of their February 17, 1912 issue. The image appears on an art print titled *Good Fellowship*.

FINNISH - K.K. OY. NO 1/20 SERIES   133

K.K. Oy. No 1/20 Series
(Mistletoe)

K.K. Oy. No 1/20 Series
(Mistletoe)
A novelty postcard with real
hair and a red satin bow.

K.K. Oy. No 1/20 Series
(Thoroughbreds)

Finnish - W. & G. American Series N:o 7001/1-35

The W. & G. American Series contains thirty-five postcards published by Weilin & Goos located in Helsinki, Finland. Five postcards have surfaced with Fisher images, others may exist. The publisher printed "W. & G. American Series N:o 7001/1-35" on the back of each card.

The postcards do not contain titles. Four images, *Alert, American Beauties, At the Toilet,* and *Following the Race,* appear on Reinthal & Newman postcards where the images receive their names. From 1910 to 1915, *Cosmopolitan* or *The Saturday Evening Post* published these four images on the covers of their magazine.

The image, titled *Yet Some Men Prefer the Mountains,* does not appear on a Reinthal & Newman postcard. The *American Sunday Monthly* magazine originally published the image on the cover of their June 1912 issue where the image receives its name.

Alert   (W. & G. American Series N:o 7001/1-35)
Published by Weilin & Goos. The image appears on a Reinthal & Newman postcard No. 763. *Cosmopolitan* magazine published the image on the cover of their October 1915 issue titled *He Won't Bite.*

American Beauties   (W. & G. American Series N:o 7001/1-35)
Published by Weilin & Goos. The image appears on another Finnish postcard within the Real Photo Type Series. The image appears on two Reinthal & Newman postcards, Unnumbered Series and Series 101. The image appears in two of Fisher's art books, *The American Girl* and *The Harrison Fisher Book. Success* magazine published the image as an illustration within their March 1908 issue.

At the Toilet   (W. & G. American Series N:o 7001/1-35)
Published by Weilin & Goos. The image appears on two other Finnish postcards, Numbered Series N:o 11 and Publisher at Polyphot American Series. The image appears on a Reinthal & Newman postcard No. 767. *Cosmopolitan* and *Nash's* magazine published the image on the cover of their November 1915 issue titled *Good-morning!*

Following the Race   (W. & G. American Series N:o 7001/1-35)
Published by Weilin & Goos. The image appears on three other Finnish postcards, Publisher at Polyphot American Series, No Identification Series, and Titled Series titled *Sport.* The image appears on a Russian postcard within the English Back Series No. 24 titled *Sport.* The image appears on two Reinthal & Newman postcards, No. 184 and No. 2088. The image appears in two of Fisher's art books, *American Girls in Miniature* and *Fair Americans. The Saturday Evening Post* magazine published the image on the cover of their November 5, 1910 issue.

Yet Some Men Prefer the Mountains   (W. & G. American Series N:o 7001/1-35)
Published by Weilin & Goos. The image appears on another Finnish postcard within the Titled Series, titled *Yet Some Men Prefer the Mountains,* where the image receives its title. The image does not appear on a Reinthal & Newman postcard. The image appears in Fisher's art book *Maidens Fair. American Sunday Monthly* magazine published the image on the cover of their June 1912 issue.

FINNISH - W. & G. AMERICAN SERIES N:O 7001/1-35 135

W. & G. 7001/1-35 Series (Alert)

W. & G. 7001/1-35 Series (American Beauties)

W. & G. 7001/1-35 Series (At the Toilet)

W. & G. 7001/1-35 Series (Following the Race)

W. & G. 7001/1-35 Series (Yet Some Men Prefer the Mountains)

Finnish - W. & G. American Series N:o 7001/36-50

The W. & G. American Series N:o 7001/36-50 is a continuation of the previous series. The series contains 15 postcards published by Weilin & Goos located in Helsinki, Finland. Three postcards have surfaced with Fisher images, others may exist. The publisher printed "W. & G. American Series N:o 7001/36-50" on the back of each card. The postcards do not contain titles. As noted in the postcard descriptions, the images appear on Reinthal & Newman postcards where the images receive their names. In 1912 and 1913, *Cosmopolitan* originally published the images on the covers of their magazine.

The Favorite Pillow (W. & G. American Series N:o 7001/36-50)
Published by Weilin & Goos. The image appears on a Reinthal & Newman postcard No. 613. *Cosmopolitan* magazine published the image on the cover of their June 1912 issue. The Cosmopolitan Print Department sold the image on a print titled *Alva*.

Girlie (W. & G. American Series N:o 7001/36-50)
Published by Weilin & Goos. The image appears on two Reinthal & Newman postcards, No. 261 titled *Girlie* and No. 2047 titled *Good Little Indian*. The image appears in two of Fisher's art books, *The Little Gift Book* titled *The School Girl* and in *Maidens Fair*. *Cosmopolitan* magazine published the image on the cover of their March 1912 issue. The Cosmopolitan Print Department sold the image on a print titled *Babette*.

A Sprig of Holly (W. & G. American Series N:o 7001/36-50)
Published by Weilin & Goos. The image appears on another Finnish postcard within the Publisher at Polyphot American Series. A variation of the image, with holly, appears on a Polish postcard within the Polish and Ukrainian Back Series. The image variation also appears on a Reinthal & Newman postcard No. 603. *Cosmopolitan* magazine published the image on the cover of their November 1913 issue. *Nash's* magazine published the image on the cover of their December 1913 issue.

W. & G. 7001/36-50 Series (The Favorite Pillow)

W. & G. 7001/36-50 Series (Girlie)

W. & G. 7001/36-50 Series (A Sprig of Holly)

Finnish - W. & G. American Series N:o 7031/1-7

The W. & G. American Series N:o 7031/1-7 contains seven postcards published by Weilin & Goos, located in Helsinki, Finland. Only one postcard has surfaced with a Harrison Fisher image. Other postcards within the series resemble Fisher's work, but cannot be confirmed because the postcards do not contain his signature, and the images have not appeared elsewhere within his work.

The publisher printed "W. & G. N:o 7031/1-7" on the back of the postcard. The postcard does not contain a title. In 1914, the *American Sunday Monthly* magazine published the image on the cover of their March issue, titled *Their Honeymoon Trip,* where the image receives its name. In 1914, Dodd, Mead published the image in Fisher's art book *Harrison Fisher Girls.* The image does not appear on a Reinthal & Newman postcard. The image appears on another Finnish postcard within the Publisher at Polyphot American Series. A variation of the image appears on a Russian postcard published by O.K. & Co. P. The Star Company sold the image on a print titled *All at Sea.*

W. & G. American Series N:o 7031/1-7
(Their Honeymoon Trip)

Finnish - No Identification Series

The four postcards within the No Identification Series have no source of identification. All of the postcards have divided backs and a dotted line stamp box, except for *Following the Race* which does not have a stamp box. The postcards do not contain titles. As noted in the postcard descriptions, the images appear on Reinthal & Newman postcards where the images receive their names. From 1910 to 1917, the images originally appeared on magazine covers for the *American Sunday Monthly, Cosmopolitan, Nash's,* or *The Saturday Evening Post.*

Autumn's Beauty (No Identification Series)
Unknown Publisher. The image appears on another Finnish postcard within the N̲o 30/25 Series. The image appears on a Reinthal & Newman postcard No. 837. *Cosmopolitan* magazine published the image on the cover of their November 1916 issue. *Nash's* magazine published the image on the cover of their January 1917 issue.

Contentment (No Identification Series)
Unknown Publisher. The image appears on two Reinthal & Newman postcards, No. 383 and No. 2050. *Cosmopolitan* magazine published the image on the cover of their February 1913 issue.

Following the Race (No Identification Series)
Unknown Publisher. The image appears on three other Finnish postcards, Publisher at Polyphot American Series, W. & G. American Series N:o 7001/1-35, and Titled Series titled *Sport*. The image appears on a Russian postcard within the English Back Series, No. 24, titled *Sport.* The image appears on two Reinthal & Newman postcards, No. 184 and No. 2088. The image appears in two of Fisher's art books, *American Girls in Miniature* and *Fair Americans. The Saturday Evening Post* magazine published the image on the cover of their November 5, 1910 issue.

The Only Pebble (No Identification Series)
Unknown Publisher. Another postcard exists with a Finnish holiday greeting overprint, "Merry Christmas", as shown on the following page. The image appears on a Reinthal & Newman postcard No. 838. *American Sunday Monthly* magazine published the image on the cover of their August 1915 issue.

FINNISH - NO IDENTIFICATION SERIES   139

No Identification Series
(Autumn's Beauty)

No Identification Series
(Contentment)

No Identification Series
(Following the Race)

No Identification Series
(The Only Pebble)

No Identification Series
(The Only Pebble)
with overprint

Finnish - Publisher at Polyphot American Series

The Publisher at Polyphot American Series contains four postcards illustrated by Fisher. Based on the similar characteristics of these postcards with the W. & G. American Series, it is likely that Weilin & Goos located in Helsinki, Finland published the cards. The publisher printed "Publisher at Polyphot American Series" on the back of each card. The postcards do not contain titles. Four images, *At the Toilet, Don't Worry, Following the Race,* and *A Sprig of Holly* appear on Reinthal & Newman postcards where the images receive their names. The image, titled *Their Honeymoon Trip,* does not appear on a Reinthal & Newman postcard. The *American Sunday Monthly* magazine published the image on the cover of their March 1914 issue where the image receives its name.

At the Toilet (Publisher at Polyphot American Series)
Published by Weilin & Goos. The image appears on two other Finnish postcards, Numbered Series N:o 11 and W. & G. American Series N:o 7001/1-35. The image appears on a Reinthal & Newman postcard No. 767. *Cosmopolitan* and *Nash's* magazine published the image on the cover of their November 1915 issue.

Don't Worry (Publisher at Polyphot American Series)
Published by Weilin & Goos. The image appears on a R & N postcard No. 614. *Cosmopolitan* magazine published the image on the cover of their March 1913 issue, and on a print titled *R.S.V.P.*

Following the Race (Publisher at Polyphot American Series)
Published by Weilin & Goos. The image appears on three other Finnish postcards, W. & G. American Series N:o 7001/1-35, No Identification Series, and Titled Series titled *Sport*. The image appears on a Russian postcard within the English Back Series, No. 24, titled *Sport*. The image appears on two Reinthal & Newman postcards, No. 184 and No. 2088. The image appears in two of Fisher's art books, *American Girls in Miniature* and *Fair Americans*. *The Saturday Evening Post* magazine published the image on the cover of their November 5, 1910 issue.

A Sprig of Holly (Publisher at Polyphot American Series)
Published by Weilin & Goos. Another postcard exists with a Swedish holiday greeting overprint "Happy New Year". The image appears on another Finnish postcard within the W. & G. American Series N:o 7001/36-50. An image variation, with holly, ß appears on a Polish postcard. The same image variation appears on a Reinthal & Newman postcard No. 603. *Cosmopolitan* magazine published the image on the cover of their November 1913. *Nash's* magazine published the image on the cover of their December 1913 issue.

Their Honeymoon Trip (Publisher at Polyphot American Series)
Published by Weilin & Goos. The image appears on another Finnish postcard within the W. & G. American Series N:o 7031/1-7. A variation of the image appears on a Russian postcard published by O.K. & Co. P. The image does not appear on a R&N postcard. The image appears in Fisher's art book *Harrison Fisher Girls*. *American Sunday Monthly* magazine published the image on the cover of their March 1914 issue titled *Their Honeymoon Trip*. The image appears on a print titled *All at Sea*.

Publisher at Polyphot Series (At the Toilet)

Publisher at Polyphot Series (Don't Worry)

Publisher at Polyphot Series (Following the Race)

Publisher at Polyphot Series (A Sprig of Holly)

Publisher at Polyphot Series (A Sprig of Holly) with overprint

Publisher at Polyphot Series (Their Honeymoon Trip)

Finnish - Pain. Karjalan Kirjap Series

This series contains four postcards published by Pain. Karjalan Kirjap located in Viipuri, Finland. The four images also appear within the Finnish Numbered Series which contains six postcards illustrated by Fisher. The postcard numbers assigned to the images are identical in both series. It is possible that the other two images in the Numbered Series, *At the Toilet* and *Welcome Home!*, also exist within the Pain. Karjalan Kirjap Series, but due to their extreme rarity they have not surfaced yet.

The publisher printed "Pain. Karjalan Kirjap. Oy., Viipuri–Suomalainen Kirjakauppa-Viipuri," and a postcard number on the back of each card. The publisher tried to remove the original postcard titles and the copyright notices from the front of the cards, but without success. With the use of a magnifying glass, the information is still readable.

As noted in the postcard descriptions three images, *Close to Shore, A Novice,* and *A Midsummer Reverie,* appear on Reinthal & Newman postcards where the images receive their names. In 1915 and 1917, *Cosmopolitan* and *Nash's* originally published these three images on the cover of their magazine. The image, titled *Playing the Game,* does not appear on a Reinthal & Newman postcard. The *American Sunday Monthly* magazine originally published the image on the cover of their September 1915 issue where the image receives its name.

Close to Shore (N:o 4)
Published by Pain. Karjalan Kirjap. The image appears on three other Finnish postcards, Numbered Series N:o 4, N̲o̲ 30/25 Series, and Otto Andersin Series. The image appears on a Reinthal & Newman postcard No. 764. *Cosmopolitan* and *Nash's* magazine published the image on the cover of their August 1915 issue titled *A Fair Breeze.*

Playing the Game (N:o 5)
Published by Pain. Karjalan Kirjap. The image appears on another Finnish postcard within the Numbered Series N:o 5. The image does not appear on a Reinthal & Newman postcard. *American Sunday Monthly* published the image on the cover of their September 1915 issue titled *Playing the Game.*

A Novice (N:o 7)
Published by Pain. Karjalan Kirjap. The image appears on two other Finnish postcards, Numbered Series N:o 7 and Real Photo Type Series. The image appears on a Reinthal & Newman postcard No. 863. *Cosmopolitan* magazine published the image on the cover of their June 1917 issue. *Nash's* magazine published the image on the cover of their July 1917 issue.

A Midsummer Reverie (N:o 10)
Published by Pain Karjalan Kirjap. The image appears on two other Finnish postcards, Numbered Series N:o 10 and N̲o̲ 30/25 Series. The image appears on a Reinthal & Newman postcard No. 865. *Cosmopolitan* magazine published the image on the cover of their August 1917 issue. *Nash's* magazine published the image on the cover of their September 1917 issue titled *A Summer Reverie.*

FINNISH - PAIN. KARJALAN KIRJAP SERIES   143

N:o 4
Pain. Karjalan Kirjap Series
(Close to Shore)

N:o 5
Pain. Karjalan Kirjap Series
(Playing the Game)

N:o 7
Pain. Karjalan Kirjap Series
(A Novice)

N:o 10
Pain. Karjalan Kirjap Series
(A Midsummer Reverie)

Finnish - Numbered Series

The Numbered Series contains six postcards illustrated by Fisher. The identification of the publisher does not appear on the postcards, but based on the numbering system it is likely that Pain. Karjalan Kirjap located in Viipuri, Finland, published the series. Four of the postcard images appear within the Pain. Karjalan Kirjap Series with identical postcard numbers. The postcards do not contain titles. All of the images, except *Playing the Game,* appear on Reinthal & Newman postcards where the images receive their names. In 1915, the *American Sunday Monthly* magazine originally published *Playing the Game* on the cover of their September issue where the image receives its name.

Close to Shore (N:o 4)
Published by Pain. Karjalan Kirjap. The image appears on three other Finnish postcards, Pain. Karjalan Kirjap Series N:o 4, No 30/25 Series, and Otto Andersin Series. The image appears on a Reinthal & Newman postcard No. 764. *Cosmopolitan* and *Nash's* magazine published the image on the cover of their August 1915 issue titled *A Fair Breeze.*

Playing the Game (N:o 5)
Published by Pain. Karjalan Kirjap. The image appears on another Finnish postcard within the Pain. Karjalan Kirjap Series N:o 5. The image does not appear on a Reinthal & Newman postcard. *American Sunday Monthly* published the image on the cover of their September 1915 issue titled *Playing the Game.*

A Novice (N:o 7)
Published by Pain. Karjalan Kirjap. The image appears on two other Finnish postcards, Pain. Karjalan Kirjap Series N:o 7 and Real Photo Type Series. The image appears on a Reinthal & Newman postcard No. 863. *Cosmopolitan* magazine published the image on the cover of their June 1917 issue. *Nash's* magazine published the image on the cover of their July 1917 issue.

A Midsummer Reverie (N:o 10)
Published by Pain Karjalan Kirjap. The image appears on two other Finnish postcards, Pain. Karjalan Kirjap Series N:o 10 and No 30/25 Series. The image appears on a Reinthal & Newman postcard No. 865. *Cosmopolitan* magazine published the image on the cover of their August 1917 issue. *Nash's* magazine published the image on the cover of their September 1917 issue.

At the Toilet (N:o 11)
Published by Pain Karjalan Kirjap. The image appears on two other Finnish postcards, W. & G. American Series N:o 7001/1-35 and Publisher at Polyphot American Series. The image appears on a Reinthal & Newman postcard No. 767. *Cosmopolitan* and *Nash's* magazine published the image on the cover of their November 1915 issue.

Welcome Home! (N:o 13)
Published by Pain. Karjalan Kirjap. An image variation, without a man, appears on another Finnish postcard within the No 30/35 Series. The same image variation appears in Fisher's art book *Beauties.* The image appears on a Reinthal & Newman Water Color Series postcard No. 387. *Cosmopolitan* magazine published the image on the cover of their April 1913 issue.

FINNISH - NUMBERED SERIES 145

Numbered Series N:o 4
(Close to Shore)

Numbered Series N:o 5
(Playing the Game)

Numbered Series N:o 7
(A Novice)

Numbered Series N:o 10
(A Midsummer Reverie)

Numbered Series N:o 11
(At the Toilet)

Numbered Series N:o 13
(Welcome Home!)

Finnish - Titled Series

The Titled Series contains twenty-five postcards issued by an unknown publisher. Harrison Fisher illustrated twenty-one, and Philip Boileau illustrated four. To date, twenty Fisher postcards have surfaced, and one image remains unidentified. The publisher printed "Stamp Here" inside the stamp box, and may have issued the series twice as the titles on the front of the cards appear in two different colors, blue and marron. All of the images, except *Dolly* and *Yet Some Men Prefer the Mountains,* appear on Reinthal & Newman postcards. Nine of the images contain different titles than their Reinthal & Newman counterparts. All of the images appear in one or more of Fisher's art books.

Be Hove! (Titled Series)
Unknown Publisher. The image appears on two Reinthal & Newman postcards, No. 302 and No. 2045, titled *Behave!* The image appears in two of Fisher's art books, *The Little Gift Book* titled *Happy Moments* and in *Maidens Fair.*

A Beauty (Titled Series)
Unknown Publisher. The image appears on two Reinthal & Newman postcards, No. 404 and No. 2086, titled *The Pink of Perfection.* The image appears in Fisher's art book *American Belles.*

Bubbles (Titled Series)
Unknown Publisher. The image appears on a Russian postcard within the English Back Series No. 9. The image appears on a Reinthal & Newman postcard, No. 403, titled *Passing Fancies.* The image appears in Fisher's art book *A Garden of Girls. Cosmopolitan* magazine published the image on the cover of their August 1909 issue.

A Dane (Titled Series)
Unknown Publisher. The image appears on two Russian postcards, English Back Series No. 12 and Real Photo Type Series. The image appears on a Reinthal & Newman postcard, No. 183, titled *Miss Knickerbocker.* The image appears in three of Fisher's art books, *American Girl in Miniature, Fair Americans,* and *A Girls Life and Other Pictures* titled *Miss Knickerbocker. Cosmopolitan* magazine published the image on the cover of their November 1909 issue.

Dolly (Titled Series)
Unknown Publisher. The image appears on a Russian postcard within the English Back Series No. 3. The image does not appear on a Reinthal & Newman postcard. The image appears in Fisher's art book *Maidens Fair. Cosmopolitan* published the image on the cover of their September 1911 issue.

Friends (Titled Series)
Unknown Publisher. The image appears on a Russian postcard within the English Back Series No. 7. The image appears on two Reinthal & Newman postcards, No. 405 and No. 2087, titled *He Won't Bite.* The image appears in Fisher's art book *American Girls in Miniature. Cosmopolitan* magazine published the image on the cover of their August 1911 issue.

Good Night! (Titled Series)
Unknown Publisher. The image appears on a Russian postcard within the English Back Series No. 19. The image appears on two Reinthal & Newman postcards, No. 259 and No. 2102. The image appears in Fisher's art book *The Little Gift Book.* *Cosmopolitan* magazine published the image on the cover of their November 1912.

Homeward Bound (Titled Series)
Unknown Publisher. The image appears on three Russian postcards, Sepia Series, English Back Series No. 21, and AWE Real Photo Type Series. The image appears on a Reinthal & Newman postcard No. 255. The image appears in two of Fisher's art books, *The Little Gift Book* and *Maidens Fair.* *The Saturday Evening Post* magazine published the image on the cover of their July 15, 1911 issue. The image appears on a print titled *A Fleeting Glimpse.*

June (Titled Series)
Unknown Publisher. The image appears on another Finnish postcard within the Real Photo Type Series. The image appears on a Russian postcard within the English Back Series No. 10. The image appears on a Reinthal & Newman postcard No. 615. The image appears in Fisher's art book *Beauties.* *Cosmopolitan* magazine published the image on the cover of their July 1912 issue. *Nash's* magazine published the image on the cover of their August 1912 issue.

Love Lyrics (Titled Series)
Unknown publisher. The image appears on another Finnish postcard within the N̲o̲ 30/25 Series. The image appears on two Reinthal & Newman postcards, No. 257 and No. 2040. The image appears in two of Fisher's art books, *The Little Gift Book* and *Maidens Fair.* *The Saturday Evening Post* magazine published the image on the cover of their August 5, 1911 issue.

A Prairie Belle (Titled Series)
Unknown Publisher. The image appears on a Russian postcard within the English Back Series No. 25. The image appears on two Reinthal & Newman postcards, No. 263 and No. 2103. The image appears in two of Fisher's art books, *American Belles* and *The Little Gift Book.* *The Saturday Evening Post* magazine published the image on the cover of their December 10, 1910 issue.

Preparing to Conquer (Titled Series)
Unknown Publisher. The image appears on a Russian postcard within the English Back Series No. 14. The image appears on a Reinthal & Newman postcard No. 256. The image appears in Fisher's art book, *The Little Gift Book,* titled *The Make-up.* *The Saturday Evening Post* magazine published the image on the cover of their October 22, 1910 issue. An image variation, with a dome, appears on a Reinthal & Newman postcard No. 2051. The same image variation appears in two of Fisher's art books, *Fair Americans* titled *Behind the Scenes* and *American Belles.*

Princess Pat (Titled Series)
Unknown Publisher. The image appears on five Russian postcards, Sepia Series (2), Real Photo Type Series No. 3223, English Back Series No. 20, and No Identification Series. The image appears on two Reinthal & Newman postcards, No. 407 and No. 2046. The image appears in Fisher's art book *A Garden of Girls.* *The Saturday Evening Post* magazine published the image on the cover of their May 21, 1910 issue. *Good Dressing* magazine published the image on the cover of their May 1913 issue.

Ready and Waiting (Titled Series)
Unknown Publisher. The image appears on a Russian postcard within the English Back Series No. 22. The image appears on two Reinthal & Newman postcards, No. 418 and No. 2092. The image appears in Fisher's art book *American Belles.*

A Rose (Titled Series)
Unknown Publisher. The image appears on a Russian postcard within the English Back Series No. 17. The image appears on two Reinthal & Newman postcards, No. 181 and No. 2089. The image appears in two of Fisher's art books, *American Girls in Miniature* and *Fair Americans,* titled *The Christmas Rose. The Saturday Evening Post* magazine published the image on the cover of their December 24, 1910 issue. The image appears on two sheet music covers titled *For You a Rose Song* and *You Withered My Roses of Love.*

Sport (Titled Series)
Unknown Publisher. The image appears on three other Finnish postcards, W. & G. American Series N:o 7001/1-35, Publisher at Polyphot American Series, and No Identification Series. The image appears on a Russian postcard within the English Back Series No. 24. The image appears on two Reinthal & Newman postcards, No. 184 and No. 2088, titled *Following the Race.* The image appears in two of Fisher's art books, *American Girls in Miniature* and *Fair Americans. The Saturday Evening Post* magazine published the image on the cover of their November 5, 1910 issue.

To Ball (Titled Series) Not shown
Unknown Publisher. The image appears on a Russian postcard within the English Back Series No. 15. The image appears on a Reinthal & Newman postcard, within Series 108, titled *The Debutante.* The image appears in Fisher's art book *American Girls in Miniature. The Ladies' Home Journal* magazine published the image on the cover of their September 1, 1910 issue titled *The Debutante Girl.* An image variation appears in two of Fisher's art books, *Fair Americans* and *Pictures in Color.*

To Walk (Titled Series)
Unknown Publisher. The image appears on two Russian postcards, English Back Series No. 2 and Sepia Series. The image appears on two Reinthal & Newman postcards, No. 409 and No. 2097, titled *Isn't He Sweet?* The image appears in Fisher's art book *A Garden of Girls. The Saturday Evening Post* magazine published the image on the cover of their August 28, 1909 issue.

To Walk (Titled Series) *Duplicate title
Unknown Publisher. The image appears on three Russian postcards, English Back Series No. 23, Sepia Series, and AWE Real Photo Type Series. The image appears on two Reinthal & Newman postcards, No. 180 and No. 2090, titled *Well Protected.* The image appears in four of Fisher's art books, *American Girls in Miniature, Beauties, Fair Americans,* and *A Girls Life and Other Pictures. The Ladies' Home Journal* magazine published the image on the cover of their February 1913 issue.

Yet Some Men Prefer the Mountains (Titled Series)
Unknown Publisher. The image appears on another Finnish postcard within the W. & G. American Series N:o 7001/1-35. The image appears on a Russian postcard within the English Back Series. The image does not appear on a Reinthal & Newman postcard. The image appears in Fisher's art book *Maidens Fair. American Sunday Monthly* magazine published the image on the cover of their June 1912 issue.

FINNISH - TITLED SERIES   149

Titled Series
Be Hove!

Titled Series
A Beauty

Titled Series
Bubbles

Titled Series
A Dane

Titled Series
Dolly

Titled Series
Friends

Titled Series
Good Night!

Titled Series
Homeward Bound

Titled Series
June

Titled Series
Love Lyrics

Titled Series
A Prairie Belle

Titled Series
Preparing to Conquer

150 HARRISON FISHER, ILLUSTRATOR

Titled Series
Princess Pat

Titled Series
Ready and Waiting

Titled Series
A Rose

Titled Series
Sport

Titled Series
To Walk (Isn't He Sweet)

Titled Series
To Walk (Duplicate Title)
(Well Protected)

Titled Series
Yet Some Men Prefer the Mountains

Finnish - Real Photo Type Series

The Real Photo Type Series contains nine postcards issued by an unknown publisher or publishers. Other images may exist that have not surfaced yet. Several of the postcards contain a title, a Reinthal & Newman copyright notice, or the words "Painted by Harrison Fisher" printed on the front of the card. All of the postcards have a divided back, but do not have a stamp box.

All of the images appear on Reinthal & Newman postcards, and several appear on other Finnish and Russian postcards. The Tin Decorating Company (Tindeco) reproduced an image variation of *All's Well* on candy tins. Photographs of the candy tins appear in Chapter 14, titled *Candy Boxes & Tins,* within *The Complete Works of Harrison Fisher* reference book.

All's Well (Real Photo Type Series) Not shown
Unknown publisher. The image appears on another Finnish postcard within the Otto Andersin Series. The image appears on a Reinthal & Newman Water Color Series postcard No. 381. *Cosmopolitan* magazine published the image on the cover of their September 1913 issue. *Nash's* magazine published the image on the cover of their October 1913 issue. The Tin Decorating Company (Tindeco) reproduced a variation of the image on candy tins titled *The Yachting Girl.*

Alone at Last (Real Photo Type Series)
Unknown publisher. The image appears on a Reinthal & Newman postcard No. 762. An image variation, with mistletoe, appears on another Reinthal & Newman postcard with the same postcard number. *Cosmopolitan* magazine published the image variation on the cover of their January 1915 issue. *Nash's* magazine published the image on the cover of their March 1915 issue.

American Beauties (Real Photo Type Series)
Unknown Publisher. The image appears on another Finnish postcard within the W. & G. American Series N:o 7001/1-35. The image appears on two Reinthal & Newman postcards, Unnumbered Series and Series 101. The image appears in two of Fisher's art book, *The American Girl* and *The Harrison Fisher Book. Success* magazine published the image as a full-page black and white illustration within their March 1908 issue.

Day Dreams (Real Photo Type Series)
Unknown Publisher. The image appears on another Finnish postcard within the N:o 30/25 Series. The image appears on a Reinthal & Newman postcard No. 848. *Cosmopolitan* magazine published the image on the cover of their May 1916 issue.

Drifting (Real Photo Type Series)
Unknown Publisher. The image appears on another Finnish postcard within the Otto Andersin Series. The image appears on two Reinthal & Newman postcards, No. 768 and No. 1000. *American Sunday Monthly* magazine published the image on the cover of their June 1914 issue.

Fair and Warmer (Real Photo Type Series)
Unknown Publisher. The image appears on a Reinthal & Newman postcard No. 842. *American Sunday Monthly* magazine published the image on the cover of their March 1916 issue.

June (Real Photo Type Series) Not shown
Unknown publisher. The image appears on another Finnish postcard within the Titled Series. The image appears on a Russian postcard within the English Back Series No. 10. The image appears on a Reinthal & Newman postcard No. 615. The image appears in Fisher's art book *Beauties*. *Cosmopolitan* magazine published the image on the cover of their July 1912 issue. *Nash's* magazine published the image on the cover of their August 1912 issue.

My Hero (Real Photo Type Series) Not shown
Unknown publisher. The image appears on a Reinthal & Newman postcard No. 977. *Cosmopolitan* magazine published the image on the cover of their July 1918 issue titled *Her Hero*.

A Novice (Real Photo Type Series) Not shown
Unknown Publisher. The image appears on two other Finnish postcards, Numbered Series N:o 7 and Pain Karjalan Kirjap Series No. 7. The image appears on a Reinthal & Newman postcard No. 863. *Cosmopolitan* magazine published the image on the cover of their June 1917 issue. *Nash's* magazine published the image on the cover of their July 1917 issue.

FINNISH - REAL PHOTO TYPE SERIES 153

Real Photo Type Series
Alone at Last

Real Photo Type Series
(American Beauties)

Real Photo Type Series
(Day Dreams)

Real Photo Type Series
Drifting

Real Photo Type Series
Fair and Warmer

French - Affiches De La Grande Guerre

Seldom seen today is Harrison Fisher's World War I American Red Cross Nurse appearing on a French postcard. Many consider this card to be the rarest and most valuable postcard Fisher ever illustrated.

In 1918, Fisher originally drew this image for an American Red Cross poster. During the First World War, he was a member of the Division of Pictorial Publicity which provided poster design services to Washington. The Red Cross was among the most active causes at that time and Fisher's nurse, reaching out her hand, became a symbol of that organization. She played a major role in their campaigns, and appeared in numerous magazines and newspapers across the country. For more information refer to Chapter 9, titled *Poster Art,* within *The Complete Works of Harrison Fisher* reference book.

Affiches De La Grande Guerre No. 11 (Poster of the Great War)
Edition des Petiles Affiches de Normandie-Rouen (Published by Petiles, Poster of Normandy, Rouen)

German - Alfred Schweizer/MEU Series

The series contains eight postcards published by Alfred Schweizer. Other images may exist. The publisher issued the postcards with three types of postcard backs. All three examples appear in Chapter 5 titled *Postcard Backs*. The first example contains Alfred Schweizer's imprint with a copyright notice by James Henderson & Sons. The second example contains Alfred Schweizer's imprint, the MEU monogram, and a Series number 4380. The third example contains only the MEU monogram.

Beatrice (Not shown)
Published by Alfred Schweizer. Two different types of postcard backs exist. One with the MEU monogram, and another with Alfred Schweizer's imprint and Series 4380, No. 9. The image appears in Fisher's art book *The Harrison Fisher Book*. The image does not appear on another postcard.

A Critical Moment (Not shown)
Published by Alfred Schweizer. The postcard back contains Alfred Schweizer's imprint, a copyright notice by James Henderson & Sons, and a postcard number 1013. The image appears on a Reinthal & Newman postcard, within the Unnumbered Series, titled *The Critical Moment*.

Final Instructions (Not shown)
Published by Alfred Schweizer. The postcard back contains Alfred Schweizer's imprint and Series 4380, No. 5. The image appears in Fisher's art book *The Harrison Fisher Book* titled *Final Instructions*. The image does not appear on another postcard.

In the Country
Published by Alfred Schweizer. Two different types of postcard backs exist. One with the MEU monogram, and another with Alfred Schweizer's imprint and Series 4380, No. 4. The image appears in Fisher's art book *The Harrison Fisher Book* . The image does not appear on another postcard.

Marcia (Not shown)
Published by Alfred Schweizer. The postcard back contains the MEU monogram. The image appears in Fisher's art book *The Harrison Fisher Book*. The image does not appear on another postcard.

On the Avenue (Not shown)
Published by Alfred Schweizer. The postcard back contains the MEU monogram. The image appears in Fisher's art book *The Harrison Fisher Book*. The image does not appear on another postcard.

Rosamond
Published by Alfred Schweizer. The postcard back contains the MEU monogram. The image appears in Fisher's art book *The Harrison Fisher Book*. The image does not appear on another postcard.

Santa Claus' First Visit
Published by Alfred Schweizer. The postcard back contains Alfred Schweizer's imprint, a copyright notice by James Henderson & Sons, and a postcard No. 526. *Puck* magazine published the image as an illustration within their December 13, 1899 issue. The image does not appear on another postcard.

156　HARRISON FISHER, ILLUSTRATOR

Alfred Schweizer/MEU Series
Santa Claus' First Visit

Alfred Schweizer/MEU Series
(In the Country)

Alfred Schweizer/MEU Series
(Rosamond)

Polish - Polish & Ukrainian Back Series

Three postcards exist with Polish & Ukrainian backs issued by unknown publishers. Due to their rarity, others may exist that have not surfaced yet. Since the placement of the printing on the back of the postcards vary, and some have divided backs and others do not, it is likely that more than one publisher issued them.

As noted in the postcard descriptions, all of the images appear on Reinthal & Newman postcards within Series 600. In 1913, the images originally appeared on magazine covers for *Cosmopolitan, The Ladies' World, Nash's,* or *Pictorial Review.*

A Sprig of Holly (Polish & Ukrainian Back Series)
Unknown Publisher. The image appears on a Reinthal & Newman postcard No. 603. An image variation, without holly, appears on two Finnish postcards, Publisher at Polyphot Series and W. & G. American Series N:o 7001/36-50. *Cosmopolitan* magazine published the image variation on the cover of their November 1913 issue. *Nash's* magazine published the image on the cover of their December 1913 issue.

A Winter Sport (Polish & Ukrainian Back Series)
Unknown Publisher. The image appears on a Reinthal & Newman postcard No. 600. The image appears in Fisher's art book *Beauties. Pictorial Review* magazine published the image on the cover of their January 1913 issue.

Winter Whispers (Polish & Ukrainian Back Series)
Unknown Publisher. The image appears on a Reinthal & Newman postcard No. 601. *The Ladies' World* magazine published the image on the cover of their January 1913 issue.

Polish & Ukrainian Back Series
(A Sprig of Holly)

Polish & Ukrainian Back Series
(A Winter Sport)

Polish & Ukrainian Back Series
(Winter Whispers)

Russian - E.K. Series

Three images have surfaced within the E.K. Series, *Dreaming of You, Maid at Arms,* and *Sweethearts Asleep*. The publisher printed their initials, E.K., and a postcard number on the back of each card. The postcard backs are divided. Additional cards may exist within this numbering sequence that have not surfaced yet. Each postcard within this series has a printing variation. For example the image, titled *Maid at Arms,* is an extremely rare hand-tinted postcard. The images titled *Sweethearts Asleep* and *Dreaming of You* are examples of postcards printed in sepia—a dark-brown or dark-yellowish pigment of color.

Sweethearts Asleep (E.K. No 3)
Published by E.K. The image appears on a Reinthal & Newman postcard No. 301. The image appears in Fisher's art book, *The Little Gift Book,* titled *Playmates*. *The Ladies' Home Journal* magazine published the image, as a full-page color illustration, within their October 1912 issue titled *Asleep*.

The Kiss (E.K. No 4) (Not shown)
Published by E. K. For a postcard description refer to page 173.

Maid at Arms (E.K. No 19)
Published by E.K. The image appears on two other Russian postcards, Sepia Series and Real Photo Type Series. The image appears on a Reinthal & Newman postcard No. 410. The colors painted on the postcard are distinctly different from the colors painted on the Reinthal & Newman postcard. The image appears in Fisher's art book *A Garden of Girls*.

Dreaming of You (E.K. No 25)
Published by E.K. The image appears on a Reinthal & Newman postcard No. 252. The image appears in Fisher's art book, *The Little Gift Book,* titled *The Siesta*.

E.K. Series, No 3
(Sweethearts Asleep)

E.K. Series, No 19
(Maid at Arms)

E.K. Series, No 25
(Dreaming of You)

Russian - O.K. & Co. P.

This rare and striking image does not appear on another Harrison Fisher postcard. A variation of the image appears on two Finnish postcards, W. & G. American Series N:o 7031/1-7 and Publisher at Polyphot American Series. In 1914, Dodd, Mead published a variation of the image in Fisher's art book *Harrison Fisher Girls*. The *American Sunday Monthly* magazine published the image variation on the cover of their March 1914 issue, titled *Their Honeymoon Trip*, where the image receives its name. The Star Co. sold the image variation on a print titled *All at Sea*. The publisher printed the wrong name of the artist on the back of the postcard. Instead of listing Harrison Fisher as the artist the card lists "Cermak" as the artist.

O.K. & Co. P., No. 2057
(Their Honeymoon Trip) Image variation
From Robert Kaplan's private collection

Russian - English Back Series

The Russian English Back Series contains a set of twenty-five postcards illustrated by Harrison Fisher and Philip Boileau. To date nineteen postcards have surfaced, sixteen illustrated by Fisher, and three illustrated by Boileau. Six more cards exist within this series, three by Fisher and three by Boileau.

Two different publishers issued the entire series, Light Publication (Orohek) and the Contragency Press. Postcards published by the Light Publication (Orohek) contain issue No. 71293, 3000 pieces printed on the back of the cards. Cards published by the Contragency Press contain issue No. 66391, 5000 pieces printed on the back of the card. The cards contain postcard numbers and titles printed on the back of each card. The title appears in two different languages, English and Russian. This is were the series receives its name, English Back Series. A print house named after Ivan Fyodorov located in Zvenigorod 11, Russia, a town near Petersburg, printed the postcards.

All of the images, except for *Dolly,* appear on Reinthal & Newman postcards. From 1909 to 1913 Bobbs-Merrill, Charles Scribner's Sons, and Dodd, Mead originally published the images in Fisher's art books.

To Walk (No. 2)
Published by Light Publication (Orohek) and Contragency Press. The image appears on another Russian postcard within the Sepia Series. The image appears on a Finnish postcard within the Titled Series. The image appears on two Reinthal & Newman postcards, No. 409 and No. 2097, titled *Isn't He Sweet?* The image appears in Fisher's art book *A Garden of Girls. The Saturday Evening Post* magazine published the image on the cover of their August 28, 1909 issue.

Dolly (No. 3)
Published by Light Publication (Orohek) and Contragency Press. The image appears on a Finnish postcard within the Titled Series where the image receives its name. The image does not appear on a Reinthal & Newman postcard. The image appears in Fisher's art book *Maidens Fair. Cosmopolitan* magazine published the image on the cover of their September 1911 issue.

Friends (No. 7)
Published by Light Publication (Orohek) and Contragency Press. The image appears on a Finnish postcard within the Titled Series. The image appears on two Reinthal & Newman postcards, No. 405 and No. 2087, titled *He Won't Bite-*. The image appears in Fisher's art book *American Girls in Miniature. Cosmopolitan* magazine published the image on the cover of their August 1911 issue.

Bubbles (No. 9)
Published by Light Publication (Orohek) and Contragency Press. The image appears on a Finnish postcard within the Titled Series. The image appears on a Reinthal & Newman postcard, No. 403, titled *Passing Fancies*. The image appears in Fisher's art book *A Garden of Girls. Cosmopolitan* magazine published the image on the cover of their August 1909 issue.

June (No. 10)
Published by Light Publication (Orohek) and Contragency Press. The image appears on two Finnish postcards, Titled Series and Real Photo Type Series. The image appears on a Reinthal & Newman postcard No. 615. The image appears in Fisher's art book *Beauties*. *Cosmopolitan* magazine published the image on the cover of their July 1912 issue. *Nash's* magazine published the image on the cover of their August 1912 issue.

A Dane (No. 12)
Published by Light Publication (Orohek) and Contragency Press. The image appears on another Russian postcard within the Real Photo Type Series. The image appears on a Finnish postcard within the Titled Series. The image appears on a Reinthal & Newman postcard, No. 183, titled *Miss Knickerbocker*. The image appears in three of Fisher's art books, *American Girls in Miniature, Fair Americans,* and *A Girls Life and Other Pictures,* titled *Miss Knickerbocker*. *Cosmopolitan* magazine published the image on the cover of their November 1909 issue.

Preparing to Conquer (No. 14)
Published by Light Publication (Orohek) and Contragency Press. The image appears on a Finnish postcard within the Titled Series. The image appears on a Reinthal & Newman postcard No. 256. The image appears in Fisher's art book, *The Little Gift Book,* titled *The Make-up*. *The Saturday Evening Post* magazine published the image on the cover of their October 22, 1910 issue. An image variation, with a dome, appears on a Reinthal & Newman postcard No. 2051. The same image variation appears in two of Fisher's art books, *Fair Americans* titled *Behind the Scenes* and *American Belles*.

To Ball (No. 15)
Published by Light Publication (Orohek) and Contragency Press. The image appears on a Finnish postcard within the Titled Series. The image appears on a Reinthal & Newman postcard, within Series 108, titled *The Debutante*. The image appears in Fisher's art book *American Girls in Miniature*. *The Ladies' Home Journal* magazine published the image on the cover of their September 1, 1910 titled *The Debutante Girl*. An image variation, with people, appears in two of Fisher's art books, *Fair Americans* and *Pictures in Color*.

A Rose (No. 17)
Published by Light Publication (Orohek) and Contragency Press.. The image appears on a Finnish postcard within the Titled Series. The image appears on two Reinthal & Newman postcards, No. 181 and No. 2089, titled *The Rose*. The image appears in two of Fisher's art books, *American Girls in Miniature* titled *The Rose* and *Fair Americans* titled *The Christmas Rose*. *The Saturday Evening Post* magazine published the image on the cover of their December 24, 1910 issue. The image appears on the cover of two pieces of sheet music, *For You a Rose Song* and *You Withered My Roses of Love*.

Good Night! (No. 19)
Published by Light Publication (Orohek) and the Contragency Press. The image appears on two Reinthal & Newman postcards, No. 259 and No. 2102. The image appears on a Finnish postcard within the Titled Series. The image appears in Fisher's art book *The Little Gift Book*. *Cosmopolitan* magazine published the image on the cover of their November 1912 issue.

Princess Pat (No. 20)
Published by Light Publication (Orohek) and the Contragency Press. The image appears on four other Russian postcards, No Identification Series, Sepia Series (2) and Real Photo Type Series. The image appears on a Finnish postcard within the Titled Series. The image appears on two Reinthal & Newman postcards, No. 407 and No. 2046. The image appears in Fisher's art book *A Garden of Girls*. *The Saturday Evening Post* magazine published the image on the cover of their May 21, 1910 issue. *Good Dressing* magazine published the image on the cover of their May 1913 issue.

Homeward Bound (No. 21)
Published by Light Publication (Orohek) and the Contragency Press. The image appears on two other Russian postcards, Sepia Series and AWE Real Photo Type Series. The image appears on a Reinthal & Newman postcard No. 255. The image appears in two of Fisher's art books, *The Little Gift Book* and *Maidens Fair*. *The Saturday Evening Post* magazine published the image on the cover of their July 15, 1911 issue. The image was sold on a print titled *A Fleeting Glimpse*.

Ready and Waiting (No. 22)
Published by Light Publication (Orohek) and the Contragency Press. The image appears on a Finnish postcard within the Titled Series. The image appears on two Reinthal & Newman postcards, No. 418 and No. 2092. The image appears in Fisher's art book *American Belles*.

To Walk (No. 23) *Duplicate Title
Published by Light Publication (Orohek) and the Contragency Press. The image appears on two other Russian postcards, Sepia Series and AWE Real Photo Type Series. The image appears on a Finnish postcard within the Titled Series. The image appears on two Reinthal & Newman postcards, No. 180 and No. 2090, titled *Well Protected*. The image appears in four of Fisher's art books, *American Girls in Miniature, Beauties, Fair Americans,* and *A Girls Life and Other Pictures*. *The Ladies' Home Journal* magazine published the image on the cover of their February 1913 issue.

Sport (No. 24)
Published by Light Publication (Orohek) and the Contragency Press. The image appears on four Finnish postcards, W. & G. American Series N:o 7001/1-35, Publisher at Polyphot Series, No Identification Series, and Titled Series. The image appears on two Reinthal & Newman postcards, No. 184 and No. 2088, titled *Following the Race*. The image appears in two of Fisher's art books, *American Girls in Miniature* and *Fair Americans*. *The Saturday Evening Post* magazine published the image on the cover of their November 5, 1910 issue.

A Prairie Belle (No. 25)
Published by Light Publication (Orohek) and the Contragency Press. The image appears on a Finnish postcard within the Titled Series. The image appears on two Reinthal & Newman postcard, No. 263 and No. 2103. The image appears in two of Fisher's art books, *American Belles* and *The Little Gift Book*. *The Saturday Evening Post* magazine published the image on the cover of their December 10, 1910 issue.

RUSSIAN - ENGLISH BACK SERIES   163

English Back Series No. 2
To Walk

English Back Series No. 3
Dolly

English Back Series No. 7
Friends

English Back Series No. 9
Bubbles

English Back Series No. 10
June

English Back Series No. 12
A Dane

English Back Series No. 14
Preparing to Conquer

English Back Series No. 15
To Ball

English Back Series No. 17
A Rose

English Back Series No. 19
Good Night!
From Robert Kaplan's collection

English Back Series No. 20
Princess Pat

English Back Series No. 21
Homeward Bound

English Back Series No. 22
Ready and Waiting

English Back Series No. 23
To Walk (duplicate title)

English Back Series No. 24
Sport

English Back Series No. 25
A Prairie Bell

Russian - Rishar 100 & 800 Series

One Fisher image has surfaced within the Rishar 100 Series, and fourteen images within the Rishar 800 Series. Other images may exist that have not surfaced yet. Rishar published both series, and Golike & Vilborg distributed them. Both companies were located in Saint Petersburg, Russia. The publisher issued the postcards with postcard numbers and with titles in three different languages, English, German, and Russian. Some of the titles appear on the front of the postcard while others appear on the back. The 800 Series contains the publisher's monogram—a circle with a soldier in the middle and the words "Richard Phillips." The two different types of postcard backs are shown in Chapter 5 titled *Postcard Backs*. As noted in the postcard descriptions six images do not appear on Reinthal & Newman postcards.

Those Bewitching Eyes (No. 117)
Published by Rishar. The image appears on another Russian postcard within the Linen Series No. 6. The image appears on two Reinthal & Newman postcards, Unnumbered Series and Series 101. The image appears in three of Fisher's art books, *The American Girl, The Harrison Fisher Book,* and *Pictures in Color by Famous American Artists*. *The Ladies' Home Journal* magazine published the image on the cover of their October 1907 issue.

Made to Worship (No. 824)
Published by Rishar. The image appears on two Reinthal & Newman postcards, No. 203 and No. 1004, with a spelling variation, titled *Maid to Worship*. The image appears in two of Fisher's art books, *The Little Gift Book* titled *The Blonde* and in *American Beauties*. *The Saturday Evening Post* magazine published the image on the cover of their October 10, 1908 issue.

In the Toils (No. 825)
Published by Rishar. The image appears on a Reinthal & Newman postcard No. 202. The image appears in two of Fisher's art books, *American Beauties* and *The Little Gift Book*. *Cosmopolitan* magazine published the image on the cover of their March 1909 issue.

Leisure Moments (No. 826)
Published by Rishar. The image appears on two Russian postcards, Linen Series No. 2 and Black & White Series. The image appears on two Reinthal & Newman postcards, No. 199 and No. 768. The image appears in two of Fisher's art books, *American Beauties* and *The Little Gift Book*. *The Saturday Evening Post* magazine published the image on the cover of their November 7, 1908 issue.

The American Beauty (No. 827)
Published by Rishar. The image does not appear on a Reinthal & Newman postcard. The image appears in Fisher's art book *American Beauties*.

Teacup Time (No. 828)
Published by Rishar. The image does not appear on a Reinthal & Newman postcard. The image appears in Fisher's art book *American Beauties*.

And Yet Her Eyes Can Look Wise (No. 829)
Published by Rishar. The image appears on another Russian postcard within the Linen Series No. 1. The image appears on two Reinthal & Newman postcards, No. 200 and No. 1005. The image appears in two of Fisher's art books, *The Little Gift Book* titled *The Eyes Under the Cowl* and within *American Beauties*.

A Taste of Paradise (No. 830)
Published by Rishar. The image does not appear on a Reinthal & Newman postcard. The image appears in Fisher's art book *American Beauties*.

Springtime (No. 831)
Published by Rishar. The image appears on another Russian postcard within the Linen Series No. 5. The image does not appear on a Reinthal & Newman postcard. The image appears in Fisher's art book *American Beauties*, and on the book cover inlay for *A Book of Sweethearts*.

Food for Thought (No. 832)
Published by Rishar. The image does not appear on a Reinthal & Newman postcard. The image appears in Fisher's art book *American Beauties*.

Lips for Kisses (No. 833)
Published by Rishar. The image appears on another Russian postcard within the Linen Series No. 72. The image appears on a Reinthal & Newman postcard No. 197. The image appears in two of Fisher's art books, *The Little Gift Book* titled *The Lady with the Fan*, and within *American Beauties*. *The Saturday Evening Post* magazine published the image on the cover of their February 6, 1909 issue.

Vanity (No. 834)
Published by Rishar. The image appears on another Russian postcard within the Linen Series No. 54. The image appears on two Reinthal & Newman postcards, No. 195 and No. 1003. The image appears in two of Fisher's art books, *American Beauties* and *The Little Gift Book*. *Pictorial Review* magazine published the image on the cover of their October 1908 issue.

Cherry Ripe (No. 835)
Published by Rishar. The image appears on another Russian postcard within the Linen Series No. 60. The image appears on two Reinthal & Newman postcards, No. 192 and No. 1001. The image appears in two of Fisher's art books, *The Little Gift Book* titled *Off to the Theatre* and within *American Beauties*. *The Saturday Evening Post* magazine published the image on the cover of their April 17, 1909 issue.

Bewitching Maiden (No. 836)
Published by Rishar. The image appears on another Russian postcard within the Linen Series No. 71. The image appears on a Reinthal & Newman postcard No. 198. The image appears in two of Fisher's art books, *The Little Gift Book* titled *Maud Muller* and within *American Beauties*. *The Ladies' Home Journal* magazine published the image on the cover of their May 1908 issue.

Polarbear (No. 837)
Published by Rishar. The image does not appear on a Reinthal & Newman postcard. The image appears in Fisher's art book, *Fair Americans*, titled *At the Fountain*. *The Saturday Evening Post* magazine published the image on the cover of their January 9, 1909 issue.

RUSSIAN - RISHAR 100 & 800 SERIES   167

Rishar Series No. 117
(Those Bewitching Eyes)

Rishar Series No. 824
Made to Worship

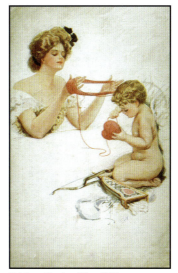

Rishar Series No. 825
In the Toils

Rishar Series No. 826
Leisure Moments

Rishar Series No. 827
The American Beauty

Rishar Series No. 828
Teacup Time

Rishar Series No. 829
And Yet Her Eyes Can Look Wise

Rishar Series No. 830
A Taste of Paradise

Rishar Series No. 831
Springtime

Rishar Series No. 832
Food for Thought

Rishar Series No. 833
Lips for Kisses

Rishar Series No. 834
Vanity

Rishar Series No. 835
Cherry Ripe

Rishar Series No. 836
Bewitching Maiden

Rishar Series No. 837
Polarbear

Russian - Linen Series

The Linen Series contains a set of eight postcards issued by the State Organization "Graphic Business," and printed at a print house named after Ivan Fyodorov located in Leningrad, Russia. Apparently, Fisher postcards were very popular within Russia, as Ivan Fyodorov's print house printed the series four times with different issue numbers: No. 52836 (10,000 pieces), No. 5350 (15,000 pieces), No. 5351 (20,000 pieces), and No. 9402 (20,000 pieces). Even though the issue number changed with each printing, the postcard number assigned to each image remained the same. Refer to Chapter 5, titled *Postcard Backs,* for a photograph of the four postcard back issues.

A unique feature about this series is that Ivan Fyodorov printed the cards on a textured linen-like card stock where the series receives its name. This feature does not exist on any other American or European Harrison Fisher illustrated postcard.

All of the images within this series appear on Russian postcards with the Rishar Series. Many postcard collectors theorize that at least seven additional images exists within this series that also exist within the Rishar Series. If this theory is correct, the missing images are: *The American Beauty, A Taste of Paradise, Food for Thought, In the Toils, Made to Worship, Teacup Time,* and *Polarbear.*

All of the images, except for *Springtime,* appear on Reinthal & Newman postcards. From 1909 to 1913 Bobbs-Merrill and Charles Scribner's Sons published the images in one or more of Fisher's art books. From 1907 to 1909 the images originally appeared on magazine covers for *The Ladies' Home Journal, Pictorial Review,* or *The Saturday Evening Post.*

And Yet Her Eyes Can Look Wise (No. 1)
Published by State Organization "Graphic Business." The image appears on another Russian postcard within the Rishar Series No. 829. The image appears on two Reinthal & Newman postcards, No. 200 and No. 1005. The image appears in two of Fisher's art books, *The Little Gift Book* titled *The Eyes Under the Cowl* and within *American Beauties.*

Leisure Moments (No. 2)
Published by State Organization "Graphic Business." The image appears on two other Russian postcards, Rishar Series No. 826 and Black & White Series. The image appears on two Reinthal & Newman postcards, No. 199 and No. 768. The image appears in two of Fisher's art books, *American Beauties* and *The Little Gift Book. The Saturday Evening Post* magazine published the image on the cover of their November 7, 1908 issue.

Springtime (No. 5)
Published by State Organization "Graphic Business." The image appears on another Russian postcard within the Rishar Series No. 831 where the image receives its name. The image does not appear on a Reinthal & Newman postcard. The image appears in Fisher's art book *American Beauties,* and on the book cover inlay for *A Book of Sweethearts.*

Those Bewitching Eyes (No. 6)
Published by State Organization "Graphic Business". The image appears on another Russian postcard within the Rishar Series No. 117. The image appears on two Reinthal & Newman postcards, Unnumbered Series and Series 101. The image appears in three of Fisher's art books, *The American Girl, The Harrison Fisher Book,* and *Pictures in Color by Famous American Artists. The Ladies' Home Journal* magazine published the image on the cover of their October 1907 issue.

Vanity (No. 54)
Published by State Organization "Graphic Business". The image appears on another Russian postcard within the Rishar Series No. 834. The image appears on two Reinthal & Newman postcards, No. 195 and No. 1003. The image appears in two of Fisher's art books, *American Beauties* and *The Little Gift Book. Pictorial Review* magazine published the image on the cover of their October 1908 issue.

Cherry Ripe (No. 60)
Published by State Organization "Graphic Business". The image appears on another Russian postcard within the Rishar Series No. 835. The image appears on two Reinthal & Newman postcards, No. 192 and No. 1001. The image appears in two of Fisher's art books, *The Little Gift Book* titled *Off to the Theatre* and within *American Beauties. The Saturday Evening Post* magazine published the image on the cover of their April 17, 1909 issue.

Bewitching Maiden (No. 71)
Published by State Organization "Graphic Business". The image appears on another Russian postcard within the Rishar Series No. 836. The image appears on a Reinthal & Newman postcard No. 198. The image appears in two of Fisher's art books, *The Little Gift Book* titled *Maud Muller* and within *American Beauties. The Ladies' Home Journal* magazine published the image on the cover of their May 1908 issue.

Lips for Kisses (No. 72)
Published by State Organization "Graphic Business". The image appears on another Russian postcard within the Rishar Series No. 833. The image appears on a Reinthal & Newman postcard No. 197. The image appears in two of Fisher's art books, *The Little Gift Book* titled *The Lady with the Fan* and within *American Beauties. The Saturday Evening Post* magazine published the image on the cover of their February 6, 1909 issue.

RUSSIAN - LINEN SERIES 171

Linen Series No. 1
(And Yet Her Eyes Can Look Wise)

Linen Series No. 2
(Leisure Moments)

Linen Series No. 5
(Springtime)

Linen Series No. 6
(Those Bewitching Eyes)

Linen Series No. 54
(Vanity)

Linen Series No. 60
(Cherry Ripe)

Linen Series No. 71
(Bewitching Maiden)

Linen Series No. 72
(Lips for Kisses)

Russian - Sepia Series

This series contains thirteen postcards printed in sepia—a dark-brown or dark-yellowish pigment of color. One image, titled *My Pretty Neighbor,* contains a small amount of color added to the card, a feature never seen before on a Fisher sepia postcard. Since the postcards have several different types of backs, it is likely that more than one publisher issued the cards. Due to their rarity others may exist that have not surfaced yet. As noted in the postcard descriptions all of the images, except *From Life,* lack the identification of the publisher, and appear on Reinthal & Newman postcards.

Bows Attract Beaus (Sepia Series)
Unknown Publisher. The image appears on two Reinthal & Newman postcards, No. 260 and No. 2102. The image appears in two of Fisher's art books, *American Belles* and *The Little Gift Book*. *Cosmopolitan* magazine published the image on the cover of their July 1911 issue.

Courting Attention (Sepia Series)
Unknown Publisher. The image appears on two Reinthal & Newman postcards, No. 422 and No. 2094. The image appears in Fisher's art book *A Garden of Girls*. The image appears on a print titled *Her Infinite Variety*.

Fine Feathers (Sepia Series)
Unknown Publisher. The image appears on a Reinthal & Newman postcard No. 408. The image appears in Fisher's art book *American Belles*.

From Life (Sepia Series)
Published by Frolov and Shourek, Moscow. The postcard was printed twice. One postcard identifies the publisher as Frolov and Shourek located in Moscow, and does not contain a postcard title. The other card is titled, *From Life,* but lacks the identification of the publisher. The image does not appear on a Reinthal & Newman postcard. The image appears in Fisher's art book *Maidens Fair*. *The Saturday Evening Post* magazine published the image on the cover of their May 18, 1912 issue.

Homeward Bound (Sepia Series)
Unknown Publisher. The image appears on two other Russian postcards, AWE Real Photo Type Series and English Back Series No. 21. The image appears on a Finnish postcard within the Titled Series. The image appears on a Reinthal & Newman postcard No. 255. The image appears in two of Fisher's art books, *The Little Gift Book* and *Maidens Fair*. *The Saturday Evening Post* magazine published the image on the cover of their July 15, 1911 issue. The image appears on a print titled *A Fleeting Glimpse*.

Isn't He Sweet? (Sepia Series)
Unknown Publisher. The image appears on another Russian postcard within the English Back Series, No. 2, titled *To Walk*. The image appears on a Finnish postcard, within the Titled Series, titled *To Walk*. The image appears on two Reinthal & Newman postcards, No. 409 and No. 2097, titled *Isn't He Sweet?* The image appears in Fisher's art book *A Garden of Girls*. *The Saturday Evening Post* magazine published the image on the cover of their August 28, 1909 issue.

The Kiss (Sepia Series)
Unknown Publisher. The image appears on four other European postcards: Danish-Uitg. de Muinck Series No. 186R, Russian-Modern Art Sofia Series No. 024 (2), and Russian-E.K. Series No 4. The image appears on a Reinthal & Newman postcard within the English Reprint Series No. 2053. The image appears in two of Fisher's art books, *Fair Americans* and *A Girls Life and Other Pictures*. *The Ladies' Home Journal* magazine originally published the image on the cover of their July 1910 issue. A variation of the image, short view with no background, appears in Fisher's art book *The Little Gift Book*. Reinthal & Newman issued the image variation within Series 108.

Maid at Arms (Sepia Series)
Unknown Publisher. The image appears on two other Russian postcards, E.K. Series No 19 and Real Photo Type Series. The image appears on a Reinthal & Newman postcard No. 410. The image appears in Fisher's art book *A Garden of Girls*.

Mary (Sepia Series)
Unknown Publisher. The image appears on two Reinthal & Newman postcards, No. 421 and No. 2095. The image appears in Fisher's art book *American Belles*. *The Saturday Evening Post* magazine published the image on the cover of their April 8, 1911 issue.

My Lady Drives (Sepia Series)
Unknown Publisher. The image appears on a Reinthal & Newman postcard No. 417. The image appears in Fisher's art book *American Belles*. The image appears on the frontispiece of a novel, titled *The Essential Thing*, written by Arthur Hodges, and published by Dodd, Mead in 1912. The frontispiece is titled *Doris*.

My Pretty Neighbor (Sepia Series)
Unknown Publisher. The only sepia Fisher postcard known to exist with color added to the image. The image appears on a Reinthal & Newman postcard No. 423. The image appears in Fisher's art book *A Garden of Girls*.

Princess Pat (Sepia Series)
Unknown Publishers. Two Russian Sepia postcards exist with the same image. One card has no identification, the other contains the Russian words "Publication II Chechina, Vladivostok"–a city East of Russia (English translation.) The image appears on three other Russian postcards, English Back Series No. 20, No Identification Series, and Real Photo Type Series No. 3223. The image appears on a Finnish postcard within the Titled Series. The image appears on two Reinthal & Newman postcards, No. 407 and No. 2046. The image appears in Fisher's art book *A Garden of Girls*. *The Saturday Evening Post* magazine published the image on the cover of their May 21, 1910 issue. *Good Dressing* magazine published the image on the cover of their May 1913 issue.

Well Protected (Sepia Series) Not shown
Unknown Publisher. The image appears on two other Russian postcards, English Back Series No. 23 titled *To Walk* and AWE Real Photo Type Series. The image appears on a Finnish postcard within the Titled Series titled *To Walk*. The image appears on two Reinthal & Newman postcards, No. 180 and No. 2090. The image appears in four of Fisher's art books, *American Girls in Miniature*, *Beauties*, *Fair Americans,* and *A Girl's Life and Other Pictures*. *The Ladies' Home Journal* magazine published the image on the cover of their February 1913 issue.

Sepia Series
(Bows Attract Beaus)

Sepia Series
(Courting Attention)
From Robert Kaplan's collection

Sepia Series
(Fine Feathers)

Sepia Series
(From Life)

Sepia Series
(Homeward Bound)

Sepia Series
(Isn't He Sweet?)

Sepia Series
(The Kiss)

Sepia Series
(Maid at Arms)

Sepia Series
(Mary)

Sepia Series
(My Lady Drives)
From Robert Kaplan's collection

Sepia Series
(My Pretty Neighbor)

Sepia Series
(Princess Pat)

Russian - Real Photo Type Series

Three images have surfaced within the Real Photo Type Series. The publisher printed a postcard number on the front of each card. Based on the numbering sequence, additional Fisher images probably exist within this series. Since the placement of the numbers and the postcard backs are identical, it is likely one publisher issued them. As noted in the postcard descriptions, all three images appear on Reinthal & Newman postcards. From 1910 to 1913 Charles Scribner's Sons published the images in Fisher's art books.

Maid at Arms (No. 3221)
Unknown Publisher. The image appears on two other Russian postcards, E.K. Series and Sepia Series. The image appears on a Reinthal & Newman postcard No. 410. The image appears in Fisher's art book *A Garden of Girls*.

Princess Pat (No. 3223)
Unknown Publisher. The image appears on four other Russian postcards, Sepia Series (2), English Back Series No. 20, and No Identification Series. The image appears on a Finnish postcard within the Titled Series. The image appears on two Reinthal & Newman postcards, No. 407 and No. 2046. The image appears in Fisher's art book *A Garden of Girls*. *The Saturday Evening Post* magazine published the image on the cover of their May 21, 1910 issue. *Good Dressing* magazine published the image on the cover of their May 1913 issue.

Thoroughbreds (No. 3270) Not shown
Unknown Publisher. The image appears on a Finnish postcard within the K.K. Oy. N:o 1/20 Series. The image appears on a Reinthal & Newman postcard No. 304. The image appears in two of Fisher's art books, *The Little Gift Book* and *Maidens Fair*. *The Saturday Evening Post* magazine published the image on the cover of their February 17, 1912 issue. The image appears on a print titled *Good Fellowship*.

Real Photo Type Series
No. 3221
(Maid at Arms)

Real Photo Type Series
No. 3223
(Princess Pat)

Russian - AWE Real Photo Type Series

Eight images have surfaced within the AWE Real Photo Type Series. The publisher printed their monogram containing their initials, AWE, inside of a small soldier's shield on the back of the postcard. The words "Post Card" is printed in two languages, Russian and Polish. The postcard back appears in Chapter 5 titled *Postcard Backs*. As noted in the postcard descriptions, all of the images appear on Reinthal & Newman postcards.

Beauties (AWE Real Photo Type Series) Not shown
Published by AWE. The image appears on another Russian postcard published by Frolov and Shourek, Moscow. The image appears on two Reinthal & Newman postcards, No. 196 and No. 1002. The image appears in two of Fisher's art books, *American Beauties* and *The Little Gift Book*.

Homeward Bound (AWE Real Photo Type Series)
Published by AWE. The image appears on two other Russian postcards, Sepia Series and English Back Series No. 21. The image appears on a Finnish postcard within the Titled Series. The image appears on a Reinthal & Newman postcard No. 255. The image appears in two of Fisher's art books, *Maidens Fair* and *The Little Gift Book*. *The Saturday Evening Post* magazine published the image on the cover of their July 15, 1911 issue.

Luxury (AWE Real Photo Type Series)
Published by AWE. The image appears on a Reinthal & Newman postcard No. 253. The image appears in two of Fisher's art books, *A Girl's Life and Other Pictures* and *The Little Gift Book*. Charles Scribner's Sons published the image in their 1913 art calendar.

Miss Knickerbocker (AWE Real Photo Type Series) Not shown
Published by AWE. The image appears on another Russian postcard within the English Back Series, No. 12, titled *A Dane*. The image appears on a Finnish postcard, within the Titled Series, titled *A Dane*. The image appears on a Reinthal & Newman postcard No. 183. The image appears in three of Fisher's art books, *American Girls in Miniature, Fair Americans,* and *A Girls Life and Other Pictures*. *Cosmopolitan* magazine published the image on the cover of their November 1909 issue.

Miss Santa Claus (AWE Real Photo Type Series) Not shown
Published by AWE. The image appears on a Reinthal & Newman postcard No. 182. The image appears in three of Fisher's art books, *American Girls in Miniature, Fair Americans,* and *A Girls Life and Other Pictures*. *Cosmopolitan* magazine published the image on the cover of their January 1911 issue. *Nash's* magazine published the image on the cover of their February 1911 issue.

Roses (AWE Real Photo Type Series)
Published by AWE. The image appears on a Reinthal & Newman postcard No. 201. The image appears in two of Fisher's art books, *American Beauties* and *The Little Gift Book*.

Vanity (AWE Real Photo Type Series) Not shown
Published by AWE. The image appears on two other Russian postcards, Rishar Series No. 834 and Linen Series No. 54. The image appears on two Reinthal & Newman postcards, No. 195 and No. 1003. The image appears in two of Fisher's art books, *American Beauties* and *The Little Gift Book*. *Pictorial Review* magazine published the image on the cover of their October 1908 issue.

Well Protected (AWE Real Photo Type Series)
Published by AWE. The image appears on two other Russian postcards, English Back Series titled *To Walk* and Sepia Series. The image appears on a Finnish postcard, within the Titled Series, titled *To Walk*. The image appears on two Reinthal & Newman postcards, No. 180 and No. 2090. The image appears in four of Fisher's art books, *American Girls in Miniature, Beauties, Fair Americans,* and *A Girl's Life and Other Pictures*. *The Ladies' Home Journal* magazine published the image on the cover of their February 1913 issue.

AWE Real Photo Type Series
(Homeward Bound)

AWE Real Photo Type Series
(Luxury)
From Robert Kaplan's collection

AWE Real Photo Type Series
(Roses)

AWE Real Photo Type Series
(Well Protected)
From Robert Kaplan's collection

Russian - Black & White Series

The image, titled *Leisure Moments,* appears on a Russian postcard by an unknown publisher. The publisher issued the postcard with no source of identification. The back of the postcard is completely blank. The image appears on two other Russian postcards, Rishar Series No. 826 and Linen Series No. 2. The image appears on two Reinthal & Newman postcards, No. 199 and No. 768. The image appears in two of Fisher's art books *American Beauties* and *The Little Gift Book.* *The Saturday Evening Post* magazine published the image on the cover of their November 7, 1908 issue. Due to the rarity of black and white postcards others may exist that have not surfaced yet.

Black & White Series
(Leisure Moments)

Russian - Modern Art Sofia Series

One image, *The Kiss,* has surfaced within the Modern Art Sofia Series. Two different postcard backs exist for the same image. The first back contains the publisher's name, Modern Art Sofia, printed in Russian, and a postcard number 024. The second back lacks the identification of the publisher, but contains the initials M.J.S. and the postcard number 024. Both backs contain Fisher's name printed as "Fischer" along with the title of the postcard translated to "A Kiss." A photograph of each postcard back appears in Chapter 5 titled *Postcard Backs*. The image appears on a Danish postcard within the Uitg. de Muinck Series, on two Russian postcards within the Sepia and E.K. Series , and on a Reinthal & Newman postcard No. 2053. The image appears in two of Fisher's art books *Fair Americans* and *A Girls Life and Other Pictures*. Reinthal & Newman issued a postcard image variation, short view, within Series 108. The same image variation appears in Fisher's art book *The Little Gift Book*. *The Ladies' Home Journal* magazine published the image on the cover of their July 1910 issue.

Modern Art Sophia Series
M.J.S. 024 and No. 024 A Kiss

Russian - No Identification Series

The author has been unable to identify the Russian publishers of the following two postcards. As a result the Russian No Identification Series is established as a way to classify the cards until additional information is obtained.

Princess Pat (No Identification Series)
Unknown Publisher. The publisher issued the postcard as a hand-tinted card with a Russian/Polish back. The image appears on four other Russian postcards, English Back Series No. 20, Sepia Series (2), and Real Photo Type Series. The image appears on a Finnish postcard within the Titled Series. The image appears on two Reinthal & Newman postcards, No. 407 and No. 2046. The image appears in Fisher's art book *A Garden of Girls*. *The Saturday Evening Post* magazine published the image on the cover of their May 21, 1910 issue. *Good Dressing* magazine published the image on the cover of their May 1913 issue.

Sweetheart (No Identification Series)
Unknown Publisher. The publisher's monogram, a circle containing a bird and two initials, appear on the back of the postcard with no other source of identification. The image appears on a Reinthal & Newman postcard No. 194. The image appears in two of Fisher's art books, *The Little Gift Book* titled *Youth* and within *American Beauties*. *The Saturday Evening Post* magazine published the image on the cover of their May 8, 1909 issue. The image appears on a collectible reproduction print advertising the Schlitz Brewing Company.

No Identification Series
(Princess Pat)

No Identification Series
(Sweetheart)

CHAPTER THREE
Overprints & Variations

Overprints & Variations

The postcards shown below contain holiday greeting overprints. Publishers added overprints to postcards to increase sales during major holidays such as Easter, Christmas, and New Years. They printed the greetings in a variety of languages, English, Dutch, Finnish, German, and Swedish. Postcards with overprints have become extremely difficult to locate, and increase the value of the card. The following page also features several postcards with image, color, and title variations.

R & N Unnumbered Series
A Fair Driver
Christmas Greetings

R & N Unnumbered Series
Over the Teacup
Xmas Greetings

R & N Unnumbered Series
The Winter Girl
New Year Greetings

R & N No. 2043
Serenade
German - Happy New Year

Finnish - No 30/25 Series
(Stringing Them)
Finnish: Merry Christmas

Finnish - Publisher at Polyphot
(A Sprig of Holly)
Swedish: Happy New Year

Finnish - No Identification Series
(The Only Pebble)
Finnish: Merry Christmas

OVERPRINTS & VARIATIONS 183

R & N No. 108
The Kiss
(image variation)

R & N No. 2053
The Kiss
(image variation)

R & N No. 256
Preparing to Conquer
(image variation)

R & N No. 2051
Preparing to Conquer
(image variation)

R & N No. 387
Welcome Home!
(image variation)

Finnish No. 30/25 Series
(Welcome Home!)
(image variation)

R & N No. 603
A Sprig of Holly
(image variation)

Finnish W&G American Series
(A Sprig of Holly)
(image variation)

R & N No. 762
Alone at Last
(image variation)

R & N No. 762
Alone at Last
(image variation)

R & N No. 838
The Only Pebble
(image variation)

Finnish No Identification Series
(The Only Pebble)
(image variation)

R & N No. 392
Gathering Honey
(color variation)

R & N No. 392
Gathering Honey
(color variation)

R & N Series 108
The Artist
(title variation)

R & N Series 108
Song of the Soul
(title variation)

R & N No. 261
Girlie
(title variation)

R & N No. 2047
Good Little Indian
(title variation)

R & N No. 771
INSPIRATION
(title variation)

R & N No. 771
INSPIRATION/Inspiration
(title/printing variation)

Finnish-Publisher at Polyphot
(Their Honeymoon Trip)
(image and color variation)

Russian-O.K. & Co. P.
(Their Honeymoon Trip)
(image and color variation)

CHAPTER FOUR
Framed Postcards

American Girls Abroad

Reinthal & Newman sold individually framed postcards from the *American Girls Abroad Series*. Reinthal & Newman mounted the postcards on a dark brown mat with a heavy cardboard backing. Printed on the cardboard backing are the words "Harrison Fisher Figures No. 580". The outer edge of the glass contains a strip of dark brown paper.

The images appear on Reinthal & Newman postcards within Series 102. The images also appear on Danish postcards within the Uitgave Louis Diefenthal Series titled *The Dollarprincess* instead of *The American Girl*.

Fisher originally drew the *American Girls Abroad* series for *The Ladies' Home Journal* magazine in 1909. The series consists of six black and white illustrations published in the interior pages of the *Journal*. Charles Scribner's Sons reprinted the series in three of Fisher's art books, *American Girls in Miniature, Fair Americans,* and *Pictures in Color*.

The American Girl in Japan
Size: 5" x 7"

The American Girl in the Netherlands
Size: 5" x 7"

The Greatest Moments of a Girl's Life

The images appear on Reinthal & Newman postcards, No. 186-191 and No. 468-473. Reinthal & Newman sold the set of postcards in a large rectangular frame commonly referred to as a postcard panel. Two different styles exist, one with the title of the image printed on a standard size postcard, and another with the title of the image printed on the mat below the postcard. Reinthal & Newman sold the postcard panels with three different titles: *The Greatest Moments of a Girl's Life, Life's Eventful Moments,* and *Six Important Events in a Girl's Life.*

    Fisher originally drew the series for *The Ladies' Home Journal* magazine in 1911. The series consists of six images. Two appear on the cover of the *Journal,* and four appear in the interior pages as black and white illustrations. The entire series appears in two of Fisher's art books, *American Girls in Miniature* and *A Girls Life and Other Pictures.*

The Greatest Moments of a Girl's Life
Postcard Panel
Size: 27 3/4" x 9 1/2"

Life's Eventful Moments
Postcard Panel
Size: 25 1/4" x 8"

The Six Senses

The images appear on Reinthal & Newman water color postcards No. 700-705. Reinthal & Newman sold the set in a large rectangular frame commonly referred to as a postcard panel. Two different styles exist, one with the title of the image printed on a standard size postcard, and another with the title of the image printed on the mat below the postcard. *The Six Senses* postcard panels are extremely scarce. They were not produced in the same quantity as *The Greatest Moments of a Girl's Life* postcard panels.

Harrison Fisher originally drew *The Six Senses* for the *American Sunday Monthly* magazine in 1915. The *American Sunday Monthly* magazine is a Sunday newspaper supplement. William Randolph Hearst inserted the supplement into six of his newspapers: *Atlanta American, Boston America, Chicago Examiner, Los Angeles Examiner, New York American,* and the *San Francisco Examiner.* The series consists of six images, all appearing in full-color on the cover of the supplement.

The Six Senses
Postcard Panel
Size: 27 3/4" x 9 3/4"

Smiles and Kisses

(Not Shown)

Reinthal & Newman produced a postcard panel titled *Smiles and Kisses*. The postcard panel contains the name of the series, *Smiles and Kisses,* printed on the original mat below six Reinthal & Newman water color postcards: *Not Yet-But Soon* (No. 384). *Smile, Even if It Hurts!* (No. 385), *Welcome Home!* (No. 387), *A Helping Hand* (No. 388), *Undecided* (No. 389), and *Gathering Honey* (No. 392). The names of the images appear on a standard size postcard, and the large rectangular frame measures 27" x 9". The *Smiles and Kisses* postcard panel is extremely rare, and seldom seen by collectors.

Framed Postcards with Poems

A rarity in any postcard collection is a Reinthal & Newman postcard, mounted in a frame, with a poem printed on the mat below the image. Three examples are shown, but others exist including *Anticipation* and *Their New Love.*

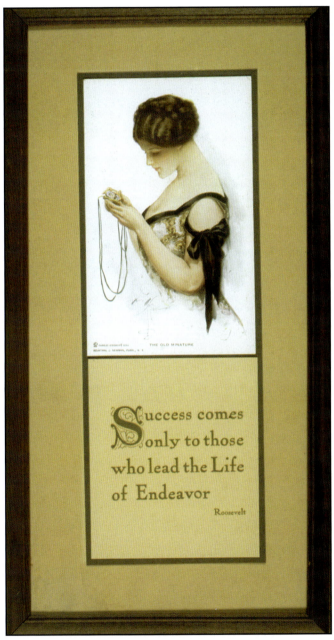

The Old Miniature
"Success comes only to those who lead
the Life of Endeavor"
Roosevelt

Size: 6 3/4" x 12 3/4"

Danger
"Drink to me only with thine eyes,
And I will pledge with mine,
Or leave a kiss but in the cup,
And I'll not look for wine."
Ben Johnson

Size: 5 1/2" x 12 1/2"

The Kiss

"This Little Paper Traveller goes forth to your door, charged with tender greetings Pray take him in. He comes from a home where you are well beloved."

Size: 5 1/2" x 12 1/2"

The Old Miniature
Size: 5" x 7"

Additional framed postcards exist without a poem underneath the image. Shown above is one example. Other images include: *A Critical Moment, A Fudge Party, Looking Backward, A Modern Eve,* and *You Will Marry a Dark Man.* Other images may exist.

The back of the frames contain a variety of information. Some have the words "Water Color Gems from the Studies by Harrison Fisher," or "Miniatures from Life, Harrison Fisher Society Sketches, Hand-Colored Series No. 727," and some lack any form of identification.

CHAPTER FIVE
Postcard Backs

American Postcard Backs

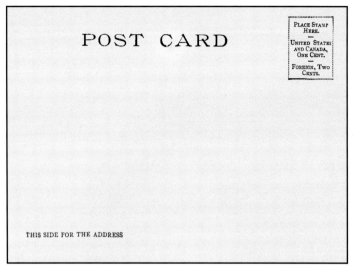

Detroit Publishing Company
Undivided Back

Detroit Publishing Company
Divided Back

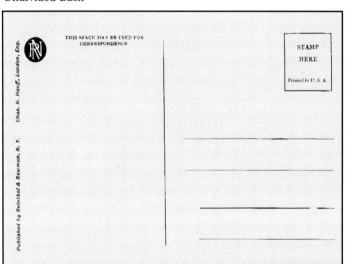

Unnumbered Series

Series 101

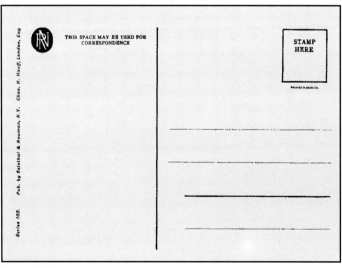

Series 102

Series 103

AMERICAN POSTCARD BACKS

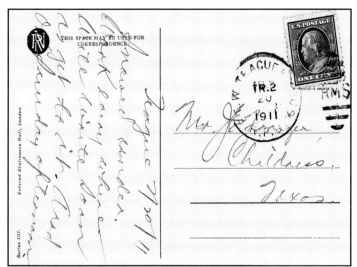
Series 107

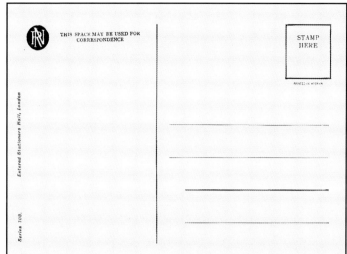
Series 108

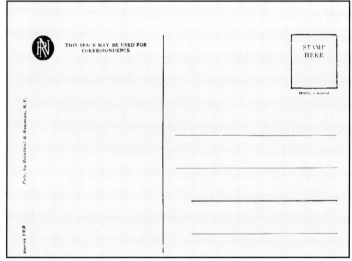
Series 123

Series 180-185

Series 186-191
Series 468-473

Series 192-203

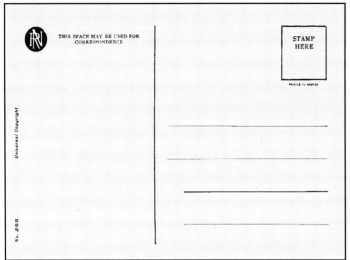
Series 252-257

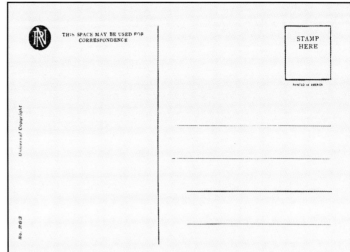
Series 258-263

Series 300-305

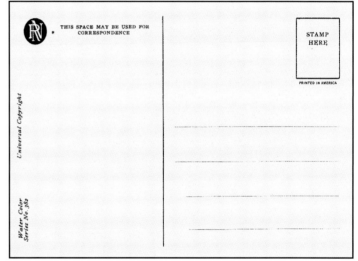
Water Color Series 381-386

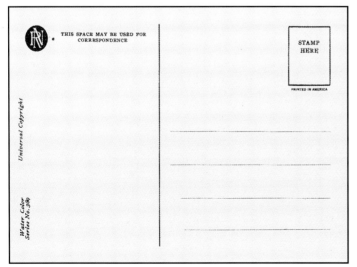
Water Color Series 387-392

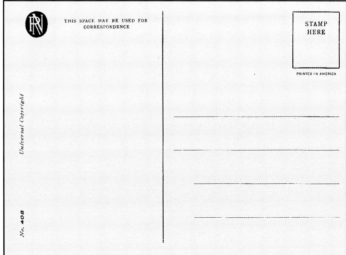
Series 400-423

AMERICAN POSTCARD BACKS 195

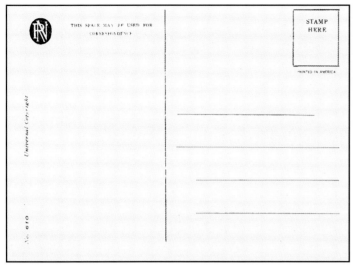
Series 600-617

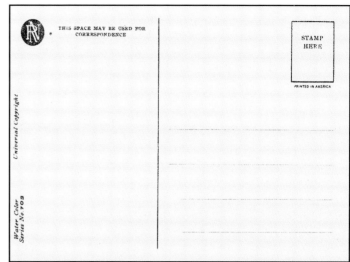
Water Color Series 700-705

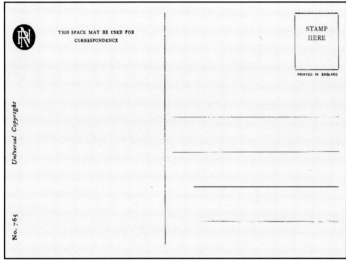
Series 762-767

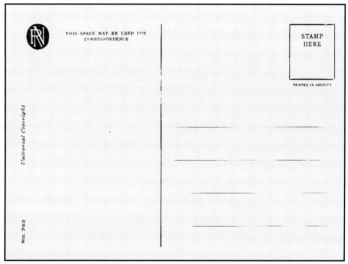
Series 768-773
With a solid line stamp box

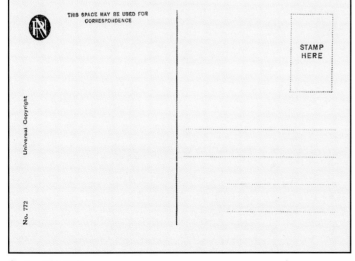
Series 768-773
With an elongated broken line stamp box

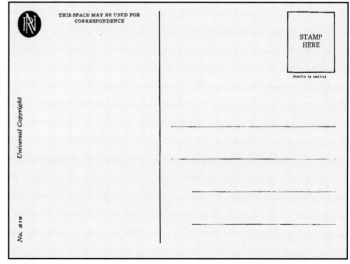
Number 819

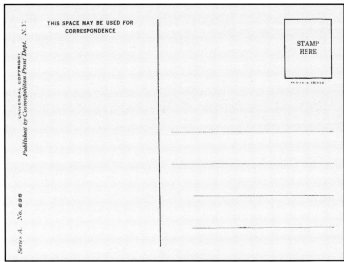
Series A, 832-837
With a series letter and the Cosmopolitan Print Dept. imprint

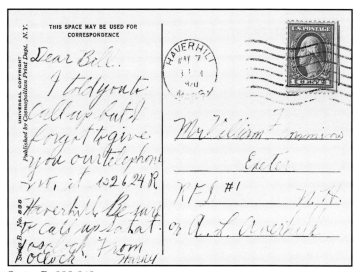
Series B, 838-843
With a series letter and the Cosmopolitan Print Dept. imprint

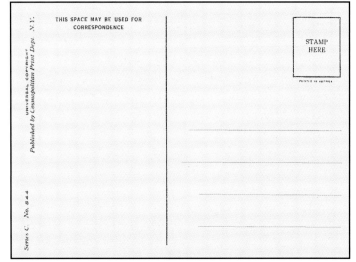
Series C, 844-849
With a series letter and the Cosmopolitan Print Dept. imprint

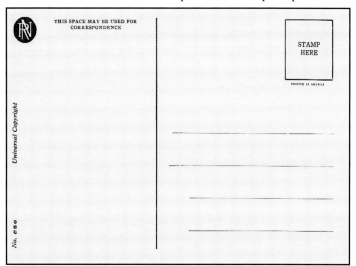
Number 856

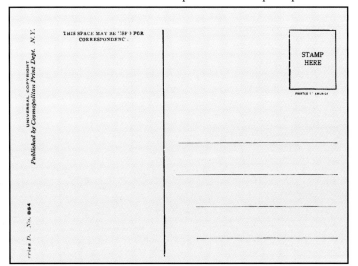
Series D, 860-865
With a series letter and the Cosmopolitan Print Dept. imprint

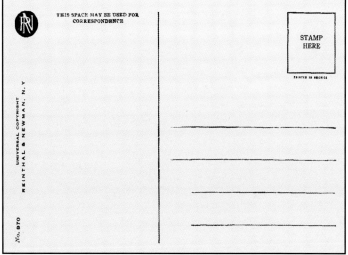
Series E, 866-871
Without a series letter and the Cosmopolitan Print Dept. imprint

AMERICAN POSTCARD BACKS 197

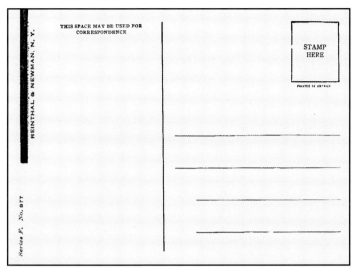

Series F, 872-877
Cosmopolitan Print Dept. imprint covered with a solid black line

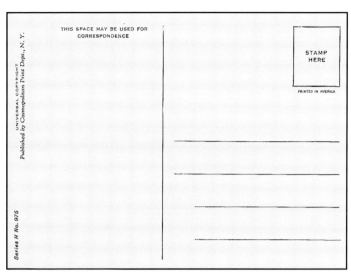

Series H, 970-975
With a series letter and the Cosmopolitan Print Dept. imprint

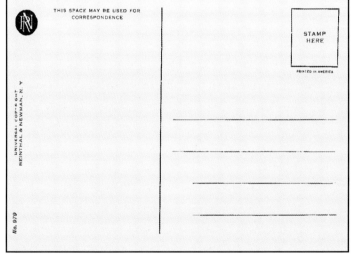

Series G, 976-979
Without a series letter and the Cosmopolitan Print Dept. imprint

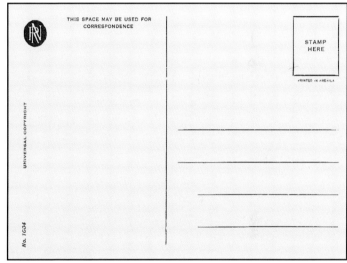

Series 1000-1005
American Reprints

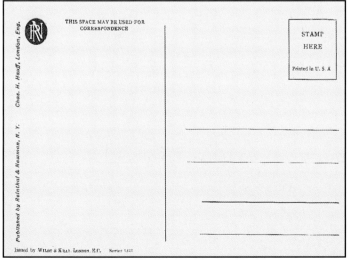

Series 1488
With Wildt & Kray imprint

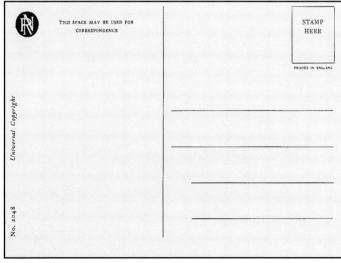

Series 2000
English Reprints

European Postcard Backs

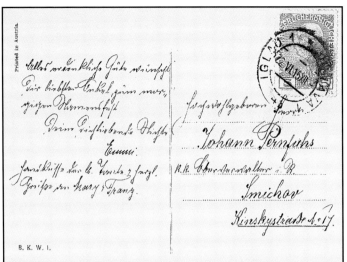

Austrian
B.K.W.I.

Bulgarian
Apollon Sophia

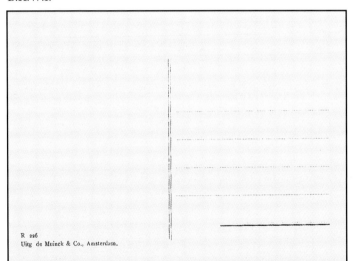

Danish
Uitg. de Muinck Series

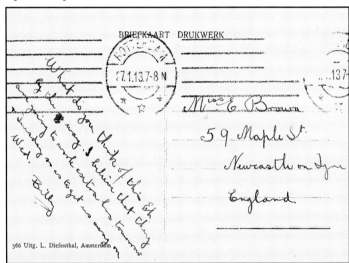

Danish
Uitg. L. Diefenthal 300 Series

Danish
Uitgave Louis Diefenthal Sepia Series

Finnish
No 30/25 Series

EUROPEAN POSTCARD BACKS   199

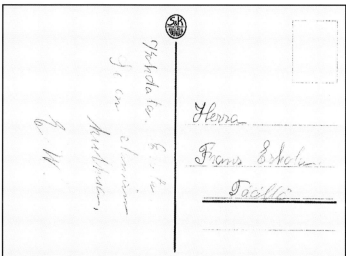

Finnish
Reversed Image Series

Finnish
Otto Andersin Series

Finnish
K.K. Oy. No 1/20 Series

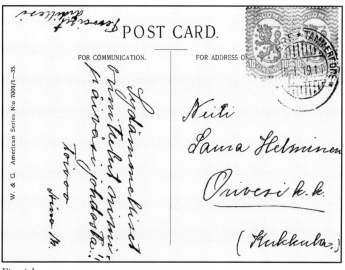

Finnish
W. & G. American Series N:o 7001/1-35

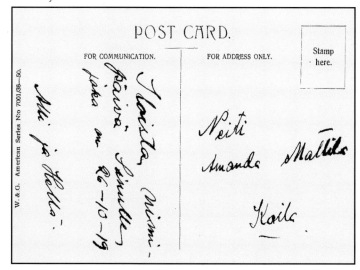

Finnish
W. & G. American Series N:o 7001/36-50

Finnish
W. & G. American Series N:o 7031/1-7

200 HARRISON FISHER, ILLUSTRATOR

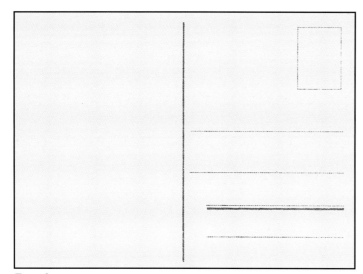

Finnish
No Identification Series (Some examples do not have a stamp box)

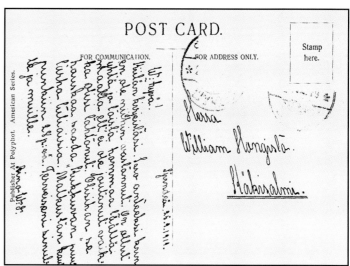

Finnish
Publisher at Polyphot American Series

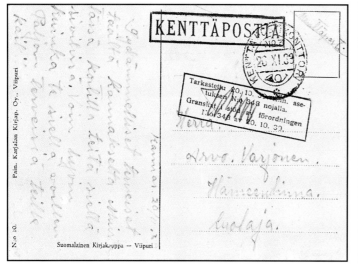

Finnish
Pain. Karjalan Kirjap Series

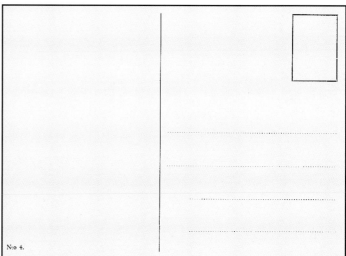

Finnish
Numbered Series

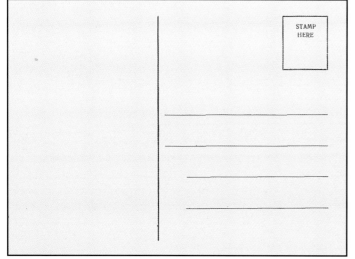

Finnish
Titled Series

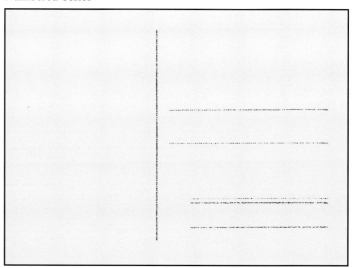

Finnish
Real Photo Type Series

EUROPEAN POSTCARD BACKS

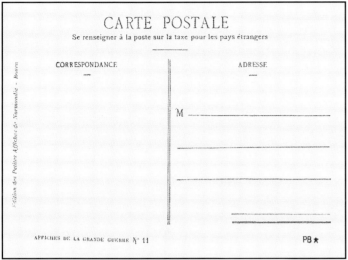
French
Affiches De La Grande Guerre

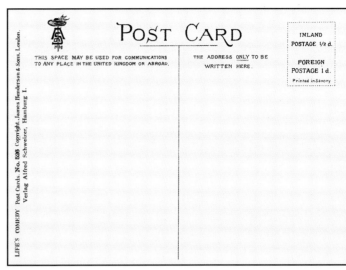
German
Alfred Schweizer (with James Henderson & Sons copyright)

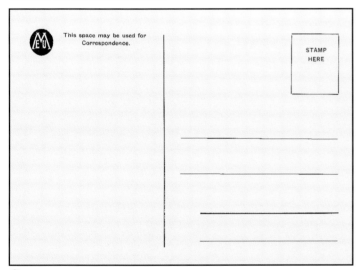
German
Alfred Schweizer (with MEU monogram)

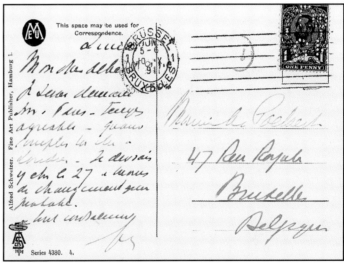
German
Alfred Schweizer (with MEU monogram and series number)

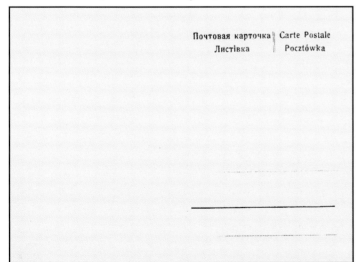
Polish
Polish & Ukrainian Back Series (postcard back variations exist)

Russian
E.K. Series

Russian - English Back Series
Contragency Press, Issue No. 66391, 5000 pieces

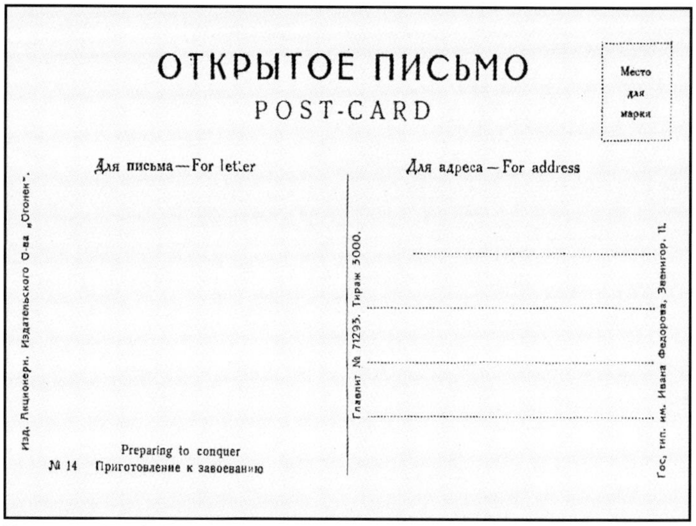

Russian - English Back Series
Light Publication (Orohek), Issue No. 71293, 3000 pieces

Russian
Rishar 100 Series

Russian
Rishar 800 Series

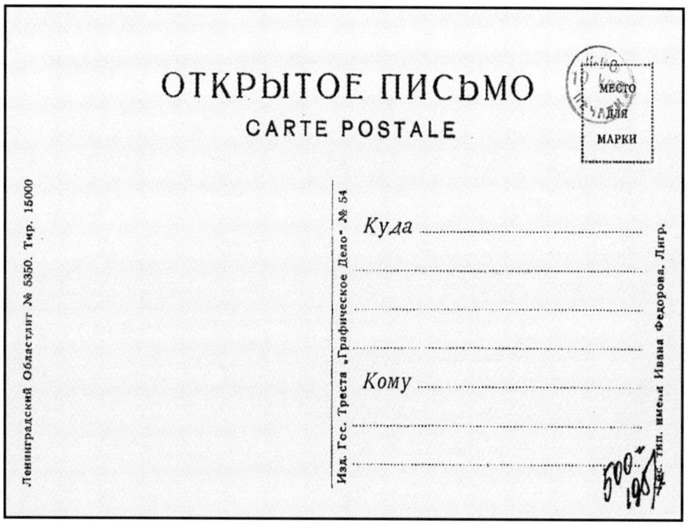

Russian
Linen Series, Issue No. 5350, 15,000 pieces

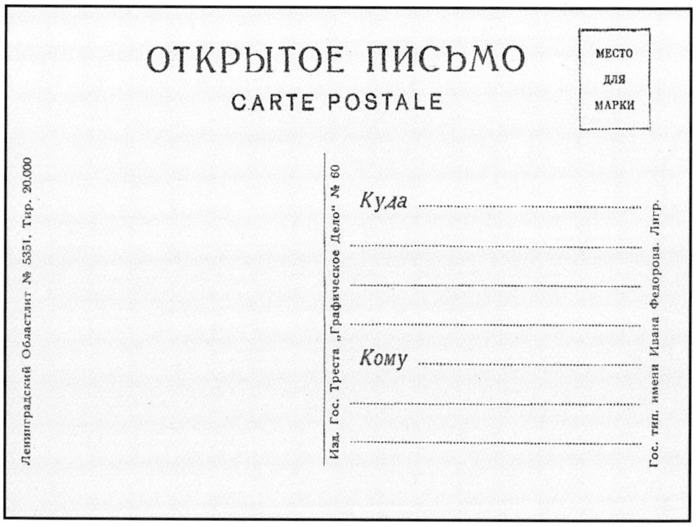

Russian
Linen Series, Issue No. 5351, 20,000 pieces

EUROPEAN POSTCARD BACKS 203

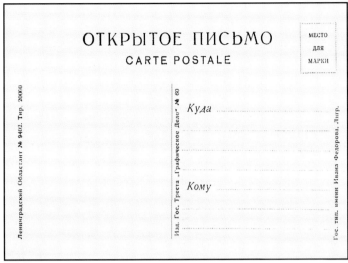

Russian
Linen Series, Issue No. 9402, 20,000 pieces

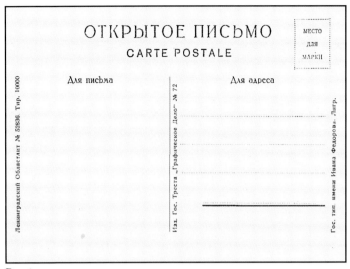

Russian
Linen Series, Issue No. 52836, 10,000 pieces

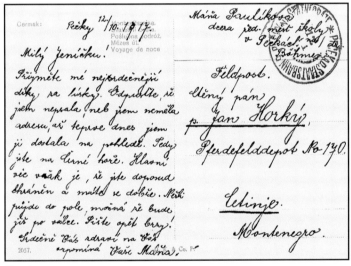

Russian
O.K. & Co. P.

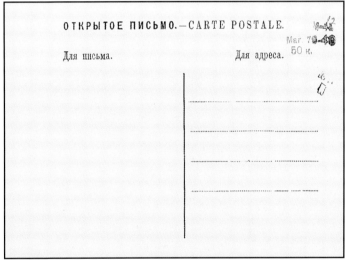

Russian
Sepia Series (some postcard backs contain a dotted line stamp box)

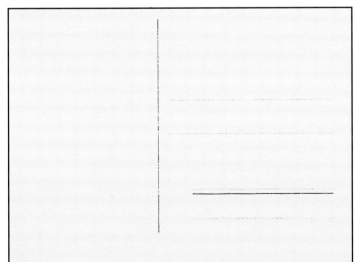

Russian
Real Photo Type Series

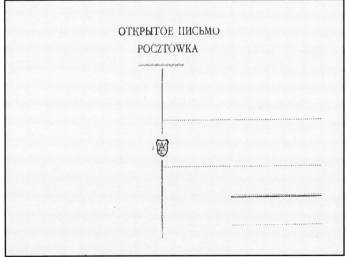

Russian
AWE Real Photo Type Series

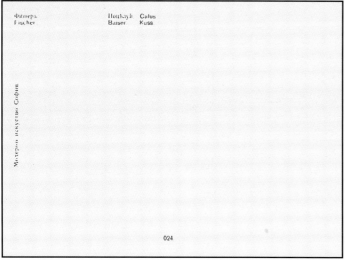

Russian
Modern Art Sofia No. 024

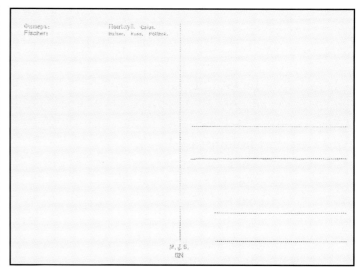

Russian
Modern Art Sophia M.J.S. 024

Index

A
Affiches De La Grande Guerre, 154
After the Dance, 29, 31, 103, 105
Alert, 80-81, 134-135
All Mine (girl holding a dog), 87, 90
All Mine! (mother and child), 62-63, 122, 126
All's Well, 64-65, 131, 151
Alone at Last, 80-81, 151, 153, 183
Ambush, 43, 45, 117-118
American Beauties, 29, 31, 40, 42, 103, 105, 134-135, 151, 153
American Beauty, 165, 167
American Girl in England, 36-37
American Girl in France, 36-37
American Girl in Ireland, 36-37
American Girl in Italy, 36-37
American Girl in Japan, 36-37, 186
American Girl in the Netherlands, 36-37, 186
American Girl's Abroad, 36-37, 186
An Hour with Art, 38-39
An Idle Hour, 122, 126
An Old Song, 43, 45
An Important Occasion, 26, 28
And shall we never meet again?, 27-28
And Yet Her Eyes Can Look Wise, 56-57, 101-102, 166-167, 169, 171
Anticipation, 33, 35, 189
Armour & Company, 11, 21-22
Art and Beauty, 68, 71
Artist, 43-45, 92, 115, 117, 184
As a beast I can destroy you and I will, 23, 25
At the Toilet, 80-81, 134-135, 140-141, 144-145
Auto Kiss, 62-63
Autumn's Beauty, 88, 90, 123, 126, 138-139

B
Baby Mine, 88, 90, 123, 126
Be Hove!, 146, 149
Beatrice, 155
Beauties
   girl holding a cat, 33, 35, 108, 111
   girl holding a dog, 56-57, 101-102, 176
Beauty, 146, 149

Beauty and Value, 60-61, 106, 109, 123, 126
Behave!, 62-63, 106, 109
Between Themselves, 26, 28
Beverly Calhoun, 11-12, 23, 25
Beverly of Graustark, 11-12, 23
Bewitching Maiden, 56-57, 166, 168, 170-171
Bill-Toppers, 18, 20
Book advertising postcards, 11, 18-20
Bows Attract Beaus, 60-61, 172, 174
Bride, 43, 45
Bubbles, 146, 149, 160, 163
By Right of Conquest, 93, 96

C
C.A. Swanson Jewelers, 11, 21-22
Canoe, 38-39, 47-48
Can't you give me your answer?, 26, 28
Can't You Speak!, 69, 72, 106, 109
Caught Napping, 93, 96, 123, 126
Chas. H. Hauff, 12
Cherry Ripe, 55, 57, 101-102, 166, 168, 170-171
Chief Interest, 68, 71
Chocolate, 75, 77, 106, 109
Christmas Belle, 73, 76
Christmas "Him", 73, 76
Chums, 98, 100
Close to Shore, 80-81, 123, 126, 131, 142-143, 144-145
Common Sense, 78-79
Compensation, 88, 91
Confidences, 88, 91
Contentment, 64-65, 107, 109, 138-139
Cosmopolitan Print Dept. catalog, 14
Courting Attention, 70, 72, 107, 111, 172, 174
Critical Moment, 29, 31, 103, 105, 155
Cynthia, 98, 100

D
Dancing Girl, 98, 100
Dane, 146, 149, 161, 163
Danger, 33, 35, 116, 118, 189
Dangers of the Deep, 83, 85
Day Dreams, 89, 91, 123, 126, 151, 153

Debutante, 43, 45, 123, 126
Detroit Publishing Company, 12, 26-28
Do I Intrude?, 69, 72
Dollarprincess in Holland, 120
Dolly, 146, 149, 160, 163
Don't you know any better?, 23, 25
Don't Worry, 74, 77, 140-141
Doris, 70, 173
Dreaming of You, 58-59, 158
Drifting, 82, 84, 101-102, 131, 151, 153
Dumb Luck, 44-45, 116, 118

E
Each Stitch a Prayer, 99-100
Engagement Days, 38-39
Evening Hour, 93, 96

F
Fair and Warmer, 88, 90, 152-153
Fair Driver, 29, 31, 40, 42, 103, 105, 182
Fair Exhibitor, 74, 76, 106, 109
Farewell, 83, 85
Favorite Pillow, 74, 77, 136
Featherbone Girl, 11, 21-22
54=40 or Fight, 18
Final Instructions, 155
Fine Feathers, 69, 71, 172, 174
First Evening in Their Own Home, 53-54, 117-118
Fisher Girl, 11, 21-22.
Fisherman's Luck, 38-39
Following the Race, 50-51, 107, 110, 134-135, 138-139, 140-141
Food for Thought, 166-167
Fore, 38-39
Forest Flower, 98, 100
Framed Postcards, 185-190
Francezka, 18
Friends, 146, 149, 160, 163
From Life, 172, 174
Fudge Party, 47-48

G
Gathering Honey, 21-22, 66-67, 184
Girl He Left Behind, 95, 97
Girlie, 60-61, 136, 184
Good Fellowship, 62, 132, 175
Good Little Indian, 106, 109, 184
Good Morning, Mamma, 74, 76, 107, 110
Good Night!, 60-61, 108, 111, 147, 149, 161, 163
Goose Girl, 18, 20

Grace Vernon, 23, 25
Greatest Moments in a Girl's Life, 14, 52-54, 187

H
Half a Rouge, 18
Handsomest man of all . . ., 23, 25
Hand-tinted postcards, 114, 120, 158, 180
Harrison Fisher Girl, 21-22
He Cometh Not, 69, 71
He Won't Bite, 68, 71, 107, 110
Helping Hand, 66-67
Her Favorite "Him", 82, 84
Her Future, 89, 91
Her Game, 87, 90
Her Heart's in the Service, 99-100
Here's Happiness, 86
He's Only Joking, 44-45
His feeble glance . . ., 23, 25
His Gift, 44-45
Homeward Bound, 58-59, 147, 149, 162-163, 172, 174, 176-177
Honeymoon, 53-54, 117-118
Hungry Heart, 18

I
I don't see why . . ., 26, 28
I fear there is . . ., 27-28
I Love You Best, 73
I suppose you lost . . ., 27-28
I'm Ready, 17, 94-96
In Clover, 47-48
In the Country, 155-156
In the Toils, 56-57, 165, 167
Indian Maid, 23, 25
Inspiration, 83-84, 184
Isn't He Sweet?, 69, 71, 108, 111, 172, 174
It's just horrid . . ., 27-28

J
J. Beagles & Co., 12
Jane Cable, 18, 20, 24-25
Jewell Weed, 19
June, 74, 77, 147, 149, 152, 161, 163

K
King of Hearts, 88, 90, 123, 126
Kiss, 44-45, 107, 110, 116, 118, 158, 173-174, 179, 183, 190
Kraus Mfg. Co., 11, 23, 25

L
La Musique, 115

Lady Tennys, 24-25
Laugh is on You!, 62-63
Leisure Moments, 56-57, 82, 84, 165, 167, 169, 171, 178
Life's Eventful Moments, 14, 187
Lips for Kisses, 56-57, 166-167, 170-171
Looking Backward, 68, 71, 191
Looks Good to Me, 80-81
Lost?, 44-45, 117, 119
Love Lyrics, 58-59, 106, 109, 124, 126, 147, 149
Love Score, 88, 90
Lucky Beggar, 95, 97
Luxury, 58-59, 176-177

M

Made to Worship, 165, 167
Maid at Arms, 69, 71, 158, 173-174, 175
Maid, to Worship, 56-57, 101-102, 165, 167
Making Hay, 47-48
Man from Brodney's, 19
Marcia, 155
Mary, 70, 72, 108, 111, 173-174
Midsummer Reverie, 94, 96, 124, 126, 142-143, 144-145
Miss Knickerbocker, 49, 51, 176
Miss Santa Claus, 49, 51, 176
Mistletoe, 132-133
Modern Eve, 47-48, 117-118
Motor Girl, 30-31, 103, 105
Muriel, 89, 91, 124, 127
Music Hath Charms, 69, 72
My Commencement, 19
My Hero, 99-100, 124, 127, 152
My Lady Drives, 70, 72, 173-174
My Lady of Cleeve, 19-20
My Lady Waits, 66-67
My Man, 99-100, 124, 127
My Pretty Neighbor, 70, 72, 173-174
My Queen, 70, 72

N

Naughty, Naughty!, 50-51, 114
Nedra, 19-20
Neptune's Daughter, 87, 90
Not Yet-But Soon, 64-65, 124, 127, 188
Novelty postcard, 132-133
Novice, 93, 96, 142-143, 144-145, 152

O

Odd Moments, 33, 35, 108, 111

Oh! Promise Me, 44-45
Old Miniature, 34-35, 108, 111, 189-190
On Summer Seas, 87, 90, 124, 127
On the Avenue, 155
One Way Out, 19
Only Pebble, 88, 90, 138-139, 182-183
Overprints, 15, 181-184
Over the Teacup
    Lady with blue hat and teacup, 30-31, 40, 42, 104-105, 181-182
    Lady drinking from a teacup, no hat, 94, 96

P

Paddling Their Own Canoe, 74, 76, 107, 110
Pals, 58-59
Parasol, 70, 72, 107, 111
Passers By, 80-81
Passing Fancies, 68, 71
Passing Glance, 74, 76
Peggy, 94, 96
Penseroso, 94, 97
Pensive Thoughts, 70
Pink of Perfection, 68, 71, 107, 110
Playing the Game, 142-143, 144-145
Polarbear, 166, 168
Postcard Backs
    American, 190-197
    European, 198-204
Postcard Panels, 187-188
Poster of the Great War, 154
Prairie Belle, 60-61, 108, 111, 147, 149, 162, 164
Preparing to Conquer, 58-59, 107, 110, 147, 149, 161, 163, 183
Princess Pat, 69, 71, 106, 109, 147, 150, 162-163, 173-174, 175, 180
Product advertising postcards, 11, 21-22
Proposal, 53-54, 117-118

R

Ready and Waiting, 70, 72, 107, 110, 148, 150, 162, 164
Ready for the Run, 30-31, 104-105
Reflections
    Lady wearing a bonnet, 34-35
    Lady holding a mirror, 94, 96, 124, 127
Refreshments, 69, 71, 108, 111
Reinthal & Newman, 12-15, 29-111
Ripening Bud, 94, 96
Rosamond, 155-156

Rose, 49, 51, 107, 110, 148, 150, 161, 163
Roses
    Lady in a chair with a rose, 56-57, 176-177
    Lady with gloves cutting roses, 95, 97
R.S.V.P., 74, 140
Ruth, 30-31, 104-105

S

Sailor Maid, 99-100
Santa Claus' First Visit, 155-156
Secret, 74, 76
Sense of Hearing, 78-79
Sense of Sight, 78-79
Sense of Smell, 78-79
Sense of Taste, 78-79
Sense of Touch, 78-79
Serenade, 73, 76, 106, 109, 182
Six Important Events in a Girl's Life, 14
Six Senses, 15, 78-79, 188
Sketching, 75, 77, 107, 110
Smile, Even if It Hurts, 64-65, 188
Smiles and Kisses postcard panel, 188
Snow Bird, 125, 127, 129-130
Snowbirds, 73, 76
So you won't kiss . . ., 26, 28
Somewhere in France, 99-100
Song of the Soul, 43-45, 92, 115, 117, 184
Sparring for Time, 88, 91
Speak!, 64-65
Sport, 148, 150, 162, 164
Sprig of Holly, 73, 76, 136, 140-141, 157, 182-183
Spring Blossom, frontispiece, 95, 97
Spring Business, 88, 90
Springtime, 166-167, 169, 171
Stooping Lady, 19
Stringing Them, 113, 125, 127, 182
Study Hour, 40, 42, 116, 118
Study in Contentment, 95, 97, 129-130
Sweetheart, 55, 57, 180
Sweethearts Asleep, 62-63, 158

T

Taking Toll, 47-48
Taste of Paradise, 166-167
Teacup Time, 165, 167
Tea Time, 74, 77, 108, 111
Tempting Lips
    Girl with feather in hat, 60-61
    Girl holding cane, 70, 72

Tennis Champion, 30-31, 104-105
Their Honeymoon Trip, 137, 140-141, 159, 184
Their New Love, 53-54, 117-118, 189
Third Party, 83-84
Thoroughbred, 30-31, 41-42, 104-105, 116, 118, 121
Thoroughbreds, 62-63, 132-133, 175
Those Bewitching Eyes, 30, 32, 41-42, 104-105, 165, 167, 170-171
Title Market, 19
To Ball, 148, 161, 163
To My Valentine, 24
To Walk (Isn't He Sweet?), 148, 150, 160, 163
Two Walk (Well Protected), 148, 150, 162, 164
Trousseau, 53-54
Two Roses, 64-65, 125, 127
Two Up, 44, 46

U

Undecided, 66-67, 106, 109, 188
Undue Haste, 55, 57
U.S. Printing & Lithograph Co., 11, 13, 21-22

V

Vanity, 55, 57, 101-102, 166-167, 170-171, 177
Variations, 181-184
Violet Book, 19

W

Wanted-An Answer, 38-39
Warren Featherbone Co., 11, 21-22
Wasn't there any . . ., 27-28
Wedding, 53-54
Welcome Home, 66-67, 125, 127, 144-145, 183, 188
Well Guarded, 66-67
Well Protected, 49, 51, 107, 110, 173, 177
What to See in America, 107, 110
What Will She Say?, 69, 72
When the Leaves Turn, 94, 96, 125, 128
Winifred, 125, 128
Winners, 94, 96, 125, 128, 129-130
Winter Girl, 30, 32, 104-105, 182
Winter Sport, 73, 76, 157
Winter Whispers, 73, 76, 157
Wireless, 87, 90

Y

Yet Some Men Prefer the Mountains, 134-135, 148, 150
You are the Keeper of My Heart, 19-20
You Will Marry a Dark Man, 47-48, 117, 119

Price Guide
&
Collector's Checklist

American & European
Postcards
of
HARRISON FISHER
ILLUSTRATOR

Table of Contents
American Postcards

Book Advertising Postcards	216
Product Advertising Postcards	216
Rare American Postcards	216
Detroit Publishing Company	217
Reinthal & Newman Postcards	
Unnumbered Series	217
Series 101	217
Series 102	217
Series 103	218
Series 107	218
Series 108	218
Series 123	218
Series 180-185	219
Series 186-191	219
Series 192-203	219
Series 252-257	219
Series 258-263	220
Series 300-305	220
Series 381-386	220
Series 387-392	220
Series 400-423	220
Series 468-473	221
Series 600-617	221
Series 700-705	222
Series 762-767	222
Series 768-773	222
Number 819	222
Series 832-849 (A-C)	223
Number 856	223
Series 860-877 (D-F)	223
Series 970-979 (G-H)	224
Series 1000	224
Series 1488	225
Series 2000	225
Overprints	226
Framed Postcard Panels	227

Table of Contents
European Postcards

Austrian
B.K.W.I. — 230

Bulgarian
Apollon Sophia — 230

Danish
Uitg. de Muinck Series — 230
Uitg. L. Diefenthal 300 Series — 230
Uitgave Louis Diefenthal Sepia Series — 230

Finnish
No 30/25 Series — 231
Reversed Image Series — 231
Otto Andersin Series — 231
K.K. Oy. No 1/20 Series — 232
W.&G. American Series N:o 7001/1-35 — 232
W.&G. American Series N:o 7001/36-50 — 232
W.&G. American Series N:o 7031/1-7 — 232
No Identification Series — 232
Publisher at Polyphot American Series — 233
Pain. Karjalan Kirjap Series — 233
Numbered Series — 233
Titled Series — 233
Real Photo Type Series — 234

French
Affiches De La Grande Guerre — 234

German
Alfred Schweizer/MEU Series — 234

Polish
Polish & Ukrainian Back Series — 235

Russian

E.K. Series	235
O.K. & Co. P.	235
English Back Series	235
Rishar 100 & 800 Series	236
Linen Series	236
Sepia Series	236
Real Photo Type Series	237
AWE Real Photo Type Series	237
Black & White Series	237
Modern Art Sofia Series	237
No Identification Series	237

Miscellaneous European   238
Overprints   238

PRICE GUIDE & COLLECTOR'S CHECKLIST 213

MARKET VALUES

The current market values in this book are for postcards in very good, excellent, or in near mint condition. Postcards in mint condition will demand higher values than those listed. Postcards in good, average, or poor condition reduces the card's value based on the card's overall condition. The market values should be used only as a guide, and are not intended to set prices which may vary from one section of the country to another. Auction prices, as well as dealer prices, vary greatly and are affected by condition as well as demand.

GRADING OF POSTCARDS

Most postcard dealers and collectors use the grading system developed by the leading postcard publication, *Barr's Postcard News*. The grading system appears below with their permission.

M - MINT
A perfect card just as it comes from the printing press. No marks, bends or creases. No writings or postmarks. A clean and fresh card. Seldom seen.

NM - NEAR MINT
Like mint but very very light aging or very slight discoloration from being in a album for many years. Not as fresh looking.

EX - EXCELLENT
Like mint in appearance with no bends or creases nor rounded or blunt corners. May be postally used or unused and with writing and postmark only on address side. A Clean fresh card on picture side.

VG - VERY GOOD
Corners may be just a bit blunt or rounded. Almost undetectable crease or bend that does not detract from overall appearance of picture side. May be writing or postally used on address side. A very collectible card.

G - GOOD
Corners may be noticeable blunt or rounded with noticeable slight bends or creases. May be postally used or writing on address side. Less than VG.

AV - AVERAGE
Creases and bends more pronounced. May be writing in margins on picture side. Postmark may show through from address side but not on main portion of picture. Corners more rounded.

PR - POOR
Card is intact. Excess soil, stained, cancel may affect picture with writing on either side. Could be a scarce card hard to find in any condition with heavy creases.

SF - SPACE FILLER
Poor condition as above and may have corners torn or corners missing etc. and breaks. least desirable of all above.

GLOSSARY OF TERMS

This price guide refers to may different terms to describe types of postcards. The terms listed below are those that relate to collecting postcards illustrated by Harrison Fisher.

UNDIVIDED BACK
The back of the postcard does not contain a vertical line. Up until February 28, 1906, postal regulations required the address be printed on the back of postcards, and the message be printed on the front of postcards.

DIVIDED BACK
On March 1, 1907, postal regulations changes which allowed the address and the message to be written on the back of postcards. These postcards have a vertical line to separate the address from the message.

ENGLISH BACK
A European postcard with words from the English language printed on the back of the card.

HAND COLORED
Color manually added to postcards after their original printing. A time consuming, labor oriented process of tinting cards by hand. These postcards were not produced in the same quantities as other postcards.

REAL PHOTO TYPE
The term Real Photo Type should not be confused with Real Photo postcards. Postcards listed in the Real Photo Type Series are postcards which resemble the appearance of Real Photo postcards.

LINEN
Postcards printed on a textured linen-like paper card stock.

REVERSED IMAGE
An image printed in reverse, and faces the opposite direction than the original source.

SEPIA
A postcard printed in dark-brown or dark-yellowish pigment of color.

WATER COLOR
A postcard printed with water colors on an absorbent buff-colored card stock.

American Postcards

THE KING OF HEARTS
© COSMOPOLITAN MAGAZINE   REINTHAL & NEWMAN, N.Y.

	VG	EX	NM
BOOK ADVERTISING POSTCARDS			
Refer to page 18-20			
Double Card	225 - 250	250 - 275	275 - 300
Single Card	150 - 175	175 - 200	200 - 225

____54=40 or Fight
____The Bill-Toppers
____Francezka
____The Goose Girl*
____Half a Rouge
____The Hungry Heart
____Jane Cable
____Jewell Weed
____The Man from Brodney's
____My Commencement
____My Lady of Cleeve
____Nedra
____The One Way Out
____The Stooping Lady
____The Title Market
____The Violet Book*

*Add $100

	VG	EX	NM
PRODUCT ADVERTISING POSTCARDS			
Refer to page 21-22			
____Featherbone Girl	75 - 100	100 - 125	125 - 150
____Fisher Girl	100 - 125	125 - 150	150 - 175
____Gathering Honey	125 - 150	150 - 175	175 - 200
____Harrison Fisher Girl	50 - 60	60 - 70	70 - 80
RARE AMERICAN POSTCARDS			
Refer to page 23-25			
____As a beast. . .	125 - 150	150 - 175	175 - 200
____Beverly Calhoun	150 - 175	175 - 200	200 - 225
____Don't you. . .	125 - 150	150 - 175	175 - 200
____Grace Vernon	125 - 150	150 - 175	175 - 200
____The handsomest. . .	125 - 150	150 - 175	175 - 200
____His Feeble. . .	125 - 150	150 - 175	175 - 200
____Indian Maid	300 - 325	325 - 350	350 - 375
____Jane Cable	125 - 150	150 - 175	175 - 200
____Lady Tennys	125 - 150	150 - 175	175 - 200
____To My Valentine	150 - 175	175 - 200	200 - 225

	VG	EX	NM
DETROIT PUBLISHING COMPANY	20 - 25	25 - 30	30 - 35

Refer to page 26-28
____14,028
____14,036
____14,037
____14,038
____14,039
____14,040
____14,041
____14,042
____14,043
____14,044

REINTHAL & NEWMAN

	VG	EX	NM
Unnumbered Series	15 - 20	20 - 25	25 - 30

Refer to page 29-32
____After the Dance
____American Beauties
____The Critical Moment
____A Fair Driver
____The Motor Girl
____Over the Teacup
____Ready for the Run
____Ruth
____A Tennis Champion
____A Thoroughbred
____Those Bewitching Eyes
____The Winter Girl

	VG	EX	NM
Series 101	15 - 20	20 - 25	25 - 30

Refer to page 33-35
____Anticipation
____Beauties
____Danger
____Odd Moments
____The Old Miniature
____Reflections

	VG	EX	NM
Series 102	20 - 25	25 - 30	30 - 35

Refer to page 36-37
____The American Girl in Japan
____The American Girl in England
____The American Girl in Ireland
____The American Girl in Italy
____The American Girl in France
____The American Girl in The Netherlands

	VG	EX	NM
Series 103	15 - 20	20 - 25	25 - 30

Refer to page 38-39
____An Hour with Art
____The Canoe
____Engagement Days
____Fisherman's Luck
____Fore
____Wanted-An Answer

	VG	EX	NM
Series 107	20 - 25	25 - 30	30 - 35

Refer to page 40-42
____American Beauties
____A Fair Driver
____Over the Teacup
____The Study Hour
____A Thoroughbred
____Those Bewitching Eyes

	VG	EX	NM
Series 108	15 - 20	20 - 25	25 - 30

Refer to page 43-46
____The Ambush
____An Old Song
____The Artist
____The Bride
____The Debutante
____Dumb Luck
____He's Only Joking
____His Gift
____The Kiss
____Lost?
____Oh! Promise Me
____Song of the Soul
____Two Up

	VG	EX	NM
Series 123	15 - 20	20 - 25	25 - 30

Refer to page 47-48
____The Canoe
____The Fudge Party
____In Clover
____Making Hay
____A Modern Eve
____Taking Toll
____You Will Marry a Dark Man

	VG	EX	NM
Series 180-185	20 - 25	25 - 30	30 - 35

Refer to page 49-51
- ____180 Well Protected
- ____181 The Rose
- ____182 Miss Santa Claus
- ____183 Miss Knickerbocker
- ____184 Following the Race
- ____185 Naughty, Naughty!

	VG	EX	NM
Series 186-191	25 - 30	30 - 35	35 - 40

Refer to page 52-54
- ____186 The Proposal
- ____187 The Trousseau
- ____188 The Wedding
- ____189 The Honeymoon
- ____190 The First Evening in Their Own Home
- ____191 Their New Love

	VG	EX	NM
Series 192-203	20 - 25	25 - 30	30 - 35

Refer to page 55-57
- ____192 Cherry Ripe
- ____193 Undue Haste
- ____194 Sweetheart
- ____195 Vanity
- ____196 Beauties
- ____197 Lips for Kisses
- ____198 Bewitching Maiden
- ____199 Leisure Moments
- ____200 And Yet Her Eyes Can Look Wise
- ____201 Roses
- ____202 In the Toils
- ____203 Maid, to Worship

	VG	EX	NM
Series 252-257	20 - 25	25 - 30	30 - 35

Refer to page 58-59
- ____252 Dreaming of You
- ____253 Luxury
- ____254 Pals
- ____255 Homeward Bound
- ____256 Preparing to Conquer
- ____257 Love Lyrics

	VG	EX	NM
Series 258-263	20 - 25	25 - 30	30 - 35

Refer to page 60-61
- ____258 Tempting Lips
- ____259 Good Night!
- ____260 Bows Attract Beaus
- ____261 Girlie
- ____262 Beauty and Value
- ____263 A Prairie Belle

	VG	EX	NM
Series 300-305	20 - 25	25 - 30	30 - 35

Refer to page 62-63
- ____300 Auto Kiss
- ____301 Sweethearts Asleep
- ____302 Behave!
- ____303 All Mine!
- ____304 Thoroughbreds
- ____305 The Laugh Is on You!

	VG	EX	NM
Series 381-386 (Water Color)	20 - 25	25 - 30	30 - 35

Refer to page 64-65
- ____381 All's Well
- ____382 Two Roses
- ____383 Contentment
- ____384 Not Yet-But Soon
- ____385 Smile, Even if It Hurts!
- ____386 Speak!

	VG	EX	NM
Series 387-392 (Water Color)	20 - 25	25 - 30	30 - 35

Refer to page 66-67
- ____387 Welcome Home!
- ____388 A Helping Hand
- ____389 Undecided
- ____390 Well Guarded
- ____391 My Lady Waits
- ____392 Gathering Honey

	VG	EX	NM
Series 400-423	35 - 40	40 - 45	45 - 50

Refer to page 68-72
- ____400 Looking Backward
- ____401 Art and Beauty
- ____402 The Chief Interest
- ____403 Passing Fancies
- ____404 The Pink of Perfection
- ____405 He Won't Bite-
- ____406 Refreshments
- ____407 Princess Pat

	VG	EX	NM
Series 400-423 (continued)	35 - 40	40 - 45	45 - 50

    ____408 Fine Feathers
    ____409 Isn't He Sweet?
    ____410 Maid at Arms
    ____411 He Cometh Not
    ____412 Can't You Speak?
    ____413 What Will She Say?
    ____414 Music Hath Charms
    ____415 Do I Intrude?
    ____416 My Queen
    ____417 My Lady Drives
    ____418 Ready and Waiting
    ____419 The Parasol
    ____420 Tempting Lips
    ____421 Mary
    ____422 Courting Attention
    ____423 My Pretty Neighbor

	VG	EX	NM
Series 468-473	25 - 30	30 - 35	35 - 40

Refer to page 52-54
    ____468 The Proposal
    ____469 The Trousseau
    ____470 The Wedding
    ____471 The Honeymoon
    ____472 The First Evening in Their New Home
    ____473 Their New Love

	VG	EX	NM
Series 600-617	35 - 40	40 - 45	45 - 50

Refer to page 73-77
    ____600 A Winter Sport
    ____601 Winter Whispers
    ____602 A Christmas "Him"
    ____603 A Sprig of Holly
    ____604 Snowbirds
    ____605 A Christmas Belle
    ____606 The Serenade
    ____607 The Secret
    ____608 Good Morning, Mamma
    ____609 A Passing Glance
    ____610 A Fair Exhibitor
    ____611 Paddling Their Own Canoe
    ____612 Tea Time
    ____613 The Favorite Pillow
    ____614 Don't Worry
    ____615 June
    ____616 Sketching
    ____617 Chocolate

	VG	EX	NM
Series 700-705 (Water Color)	30 - 35	35 - 40	40 - 45

Refer to page 78-79
- ___700 Sense of Sight
- ___701 Sense of Smell
- ___702 Sense of Taste
- ___703 Sense of Hearing
- ___704 Sense of Touch
- ___705 Common Sense

	VG	EX	NM
Series 762-767	20 - 25	25 - 30	30 - 35

Refer to page 80-81
- ___762 Alone at Last
- ___763 Alert
- ___764 Close to Shore
- ___765 Looks Good to Me
- ___766 Passers By
- ___767 At the Toilet

Series 768-773

	VG	EX	NM
Without German Captions	20 - 25	25 - 30	30 - 35

Refer to page 82-85
- ___768 Leisure Moments
- ___768 Drifting
- ___769 Her Favorite "Him"
- ___770 The Third Party
- ___771 Inspiration
- ___771 INSPIRATION/Inspiration
- ___772 Dangers of the Deep
- ___773 Farewell

Series 768-773

	VG	EX	NM
With German Cations	30 - 35	35 - 40	40 - 45

Refer to page 82-85
- ___768 Her Favorite "Him"
- ___769 Drifting
- ___770 The Third Party
- ___771 Inspiration
- ___772 Dangers of the Deep
- ___773 Farewell

	VG	EX	NM
Number 819	20 - 25	25 - 30	30 - 35

Refer to page 86
- ___819 Here's Happiness

	VG	EX	NM
Series 832-837 (A)	30 - 35	35 - 40	40 - 45

Refer to page 87-90
- ____832 Wireless
- ____833 Neptune's Daughter
- ____834 Her Game
- ____835 All Mine
- ____836 On Summer Seas
- ____837 Autumn's Beauty

	VG	EX	NM
Series 838-843 (B)	30 - 35	35 - 40	40 - 45

Refer to page 87-90
- ____838 The Only Pebble
- ____839 A Love Score
- ____840 Spring Business
- ____841 The King of Hearts
- ____842 Fair and Warmer
- ____843 Baby Mine

	VG	EX	NM
Series 844-849 (C)	35 - 40	40 - 45	45 - 50

Refer to page 87-91
- ____844 Compensation
- ____845 Sparring for Time
- ____846 Confidences
- ____847 Her Future
- ____848 Day Dreams
- ____849 Muriel

	VG	EX	NM
Number 856	25 - 30	30 - 35	35 - 40

Refer to page 92
- ____856 The Song of the Soul

	VG	EX	NM
Series 860-865 (D)	35 - 40	40 - 45	45 - 50

Refer to page 93-96
- ____860 By Right of Conquest
- ____861 The Evening Hour
- ____862 Caught Napping
- ____863 A Novice
- ____864 Winners
- ____865 A Midsummer Reverie

	VG	EX	NM
Series 866-871 (E)	30 - 35	35 - 40	40 - 45

Refer to page 93-96
- ____866 When the Leaves Turn
- ____867 Over the Teacup
- ____868 A Ripening Bud
- ____869 I'm Ready*
- ____870 Reflections
- ____871 Peggy

*Add $25

	VG	EX	NM
Series 872-877 (F)	30 - 35	35 - 40	40 - 45

Refer to page 93-97
- ____872 Penseroso
- ____873 The Girl He Left Behind
- ____874 A Spring Blossom
- ____875 A Study in Contentment
- ____876 A Lucky Beggar
- ____877 Roses

	VG	EX	NM
Series 970-975 (H)	125 - 150	150 - 175	175 - 200

Refer to page 98-100
- ____970 Chums
- ____971 Cynthia
- ____972 A Forest Flower
- ____973 The Dancing Girl
- ____974 Each Stitch a Prayer*
- ____975 The Sailor Maid*

*Add $25

Note: Postcards within this series were also printed with a Series letter G.

	VG	EX	NM
Series 976-979 (G)	150 - 175	175 - 200	200 - 225

Refer to page 98-100
- ____976 My Man
- ____977 My Hero
- ____978 Her Heart's in the Service
- ____979 Somewhere in France

	VG	EX	NM
Series 1000 American Reprints	25 - 30	30 - 35	35 - 40

Refer to page 101-102
- ____1000 Drifting
- ____1001 Cherry Ripe
- ____1002 Beauties
- ____1003 Vanity
- ____1004 Maid to Worship
- ____1005 And Yet Her Eyes Can Look Wise

	VG	EX	NM
Series 1488	30 - 35	35 - 40	40 - 45

Refer to page 103-105
____After the Dance
____American Beauties
____The Critical Moment
____A Fair Driver
____The Motor Girl
____Over the Teacup
____Ready for the Run
____Ruth
____A Tennis Champion
____A Thoroughbred
____Those Bewitching Eyes
____The Winter Girl

Series 2000
English Reprints　　　　　25 - 30　　　30 - 35　　　35 - 40
Refer to page 106-111
____2040 Love Lyrics
____2041 Fair Exhibitor*
____2042 Can't You Speak?*
____2043 Serenade*
____2044 Undecided
____2045 Behave!
____2046 Princess Pat*
____2047 Good Little Indian
____2048 Chocolate*
____2049 Beauty and Value
____2050 Contentment
____2051 Preparing to Conquer
____2053 The Kiss
____2054 What to See in America
____2069 Paddling Their Own Canoe*
____2076 Good Morning, Mamma*
____2086 The Pink of Perfection*
____2087 He Won't Bite-*
____2088 Following the Race
____2089 The Rose
____2090 Well Protected
____2091 Sketching*
____2092 Ready and Waiting*
____2093 The Parasol*
____2094 Courting Attention*
____2095 Mary*
____2096 Refreshments*
____2097 Isn't He Sweet?*

	VG	EX	NM
Series 2000 (continued)	25 - 30	30 - 35	35 - 40

English Reprints
____2098 The Old Miniature
____2099 Beauties
____2100 Odd Moments
____2101 Tea Time*
____2102 Good Night!
____2103 A Prairie Belle
*Add $10

Overprints
Refer to page 182

	VG	EX	NM
____American Beauties Unnumbered Series	65 - 70	70 - 75	75 - 80
____Chocolate No. 617	85 - 90	90 - 95	95 - 100
____A Fair Driver Unnumbered Series	65 - 70	70 - 75	75 - 80
____In the Toils No. 202	70 - 75	75 - 80	80 - 85
____Over the Teacup Unnumbered Series	65 - 70	70 - 75	75 - 80
____Serenade No. 2043	85 - 90	90 - 95	95 - 100
____The Winter Girl Unnumbered Series	65 - 70	70 - 75	75 - 80
____A Winter Sport No. 600	85 - 90	90 - 95	95 - 100
____Winter Whispers No. 601	85 - 90	90 - 95	95 - 100

____Others (add $50 to the market value of the postcard)

	VG	EX	NM
Framed Postcards			
Refer to page 186			
American Girls Abroad Series	30 - 35	35 - 40	40 - 45
____The American Girl in Japan			
____The American Girl in England			
____The American Girl in Ireland			
____The American Girl in Italy			
____The American Girl in France			
____The American Girl in The Netherlands			
Framed Postcards	30 - 35	35 - 40	40 - 45
Refer to page 190			
____A Critical Moment			
____A Fudge Party			
____Looking Backward*			
____A Modern Eve			
____The Old Miniature			
____You Will Marry A Dark Man			
____Others			
*Add $20			
Framed Postcards with Poems	45 - 50	50 - 55	55 - 60
Refer to page 189-190			
____Anticipation			
____Danger			
____The Kiss			
____The Old Miniature			
Framed Art Prints with Poems	75 -100	100-125	125-150
____Their New Love			
Postcard Panels			
Refer to page 187-188			
____The Greatest Moments of a Girl's Life	275	300	325
____Life's Eventful Moments	300	325	350
____Six Important Events in a Girl's Life	300	325	350
____The Six Senses	325	350	375
____Smiles and Kisses	350	375	400

European Postcards

	VG	EX	NM

Austrian
B.K.W.I.   125 - 150   150 - 175   175 - 200
Refer to page 114
____Naughty, Naughty!

Bulgarian
Apollon Sophia   100 - 125   125 - 150   150 - 175
Refer to page 115
____La Musique (Music)

Danish
Uitg. de Muinck Series   150 - 175   175 - 200   200 - 225
Refer to page 116-119
____R 185 The Kiss
____186 R The Kiss
____R 188 Dumb Luck
____R 191 Danger
____R 192 A Study Hour
____R 193 Thoroughbred
____R 197 The Ambush
____R 223 The Proposal
____R 224 The Honeymoon
____R 225 The First Evening in Their New Home
____R 226 Their New Love
____R 231 A Modern Eve
____R 232 Lost?
____R 233 You Will Marry a Dark Man

Danish
Uitg. L. Diefenthal   175 - 200   200 - 225   225 - 250
300 Series
Refer to page 120
____366 The Dollarprincess in Holland (Hand-Tinted)
____366 The Dollarprincess in Holland (Black & White)

Danish
Uitgave Louis Diefenthal   150 - 175   175 - 200   200 - 225
Sepia Series
Refer to page 121
____A Thoroughbred

	VG	EX	NM

Finnish
No 30/25 Series   125 - 150   150 - 175   175 - 200
Refer to page 122-128
    ____An Idle Hour*
    ____Autumn's Beauty
    ____Baby Mine
    ____The King of Hearts
    ____Love Lyrics
    ____Muriel
    ____My Hero
    ____My Man
    ____Not Yet-But Soon
    ____When the Leaves Turn
    ____All Mine!   150 - 175   175 - 200   200 - 225
    ____Beauty and Value
    ____Caught Napping
    ____Close to Shore
    ____Day Dreams
    ____On Summer Seas
    ____Reflections
    ____Two Roses
    ____Winifred*
    ____Winners
    ____Stringing Them*   175 - 200   200 - 225   225 - 250
    ____A Midsummer Reverie   200 - 225   225 - 250   250 - 275
    ____Welcome Home! (variation)*
    ____The Debutante*   225 - 250   250 - 275   275 - 300
    ____The Snow Bird*
For unsigned postcards add $25
*Image does not appear on a Reinthal & Newman postcard.

Finnish
Reversed Image Series   300 - 325   325 - 350   350 - 375
Refer to page 129-130
    ____The Snow Bird*
    ____A Study in Contentment
    ____Winners
*Image does not appear on a Reinthal & Newman postcard, add $25.

Finnish
Otto Andersin Series   350 - 375   375 - 400   400 - 425
Refer to page 131
    ____All's Well
    ____Close to Shore
    ____Drifting

	VG	EX	NM

Finnish
K.K. Oy. No 1/20 Series   200 - 225   225 - 250   250 - 275
Refer to page 132-133
____Mistletoe*
____Mistletoe (novelty)*
____Thoroughbreds

*Image does not appear on a Reinthal & Newman postcard, add $50.

Finnish
W. & G. American Series
N:o 7001/1-35   200 - 225   225 - 250   250 - 275
Refer to page 134-135
____Alert
____American Beauties
____At the Toilet
____Following the Race
____Yet Some Men Prefer the Mountains*

*Image does not appear on a Reinthal & Newman postcard, add $25.

Finnish
W. & G. American Series
N:o 7001/36-50   200 - 225   225 - 250   250 - 275
Refer to page 136
____The Favorite Pillow
____Girlie
____A Sprig of Holly (variation)*

*Image does not appear on a Reinthal & Newman postcard, add $25.

Finnish
W. & G. American Series
N:o 7031/1-7   225 - 250   250 - 275   275 - 300
Refer to page 137
____Their Honeymoon Trip*

*Image does not appear on a Reinthal & Newman postcard.

Finnish
No Identification Series   200 - 225   225 - 250   250 - 300
Refer to page 138-139
____Autumn's Beauty
____Contentment
____Following the Race
____The Only Pebble

	VG	EX	NM

Finnish
Publisher at Polyphot American Series
Refer to page 140-141   175 - 200   200 - 225   225 - 250
____At the Toilet
____Don't Worry
____Following the Race
____A Sprig of Holly (variation)*
____Their Honeymoon Trip*
*Image does not appear on a Reinthal & Newman postcard, add $50.

Finnish
Pain. Karjalan Kirjap Series   200 - 225   225 - 250   250 - 275
Refer to page 142-143
____N:o 4   Close to Shore
____N:o 5   Playing the Game*
____N:o 7   A Novice
____N:o 10 A Midsummer Reverie
*Image does not appear on a Reinthal & Newman postcard, add $50.

Finnish
Numbered Series   200 - 225   225 - 250   250 - 275
Refer to page 144-145
____N:o 4   Close to Shore
____N:o 5   Playing the Game*
____N:o 7   A Novice
____N:o 10 A Midsummer Reverie**
____N:o 11 At the Toilet
____N:0 13 Welcome Home!
*Image does not appear on a Reinthal & Newman postcard, add $50.
**Add $50

Finnish
Titled Series   150 - 175   175 - 200   200 - 225
Refer to page 146-150
____Be Hove!
____A Beauty
____Bubbles
____A Dane
____Dolly*
____Friends
____Good Night!
____Homeward Bound
____June
____Love Lyrics
____A Prairie Belle
____Preparing to Conquer

	VG	EX	NM
Titled Series (continued)	150 - 175	175 - 200	200 - 225

____Princess Pat
____Ready and Waiting
____A Rose
____Sport
____To Ball
____To Walk (Isn't He Sweet?)
____To Walk (Well Protected)
____Yet Some Men Prefer the Mountains*

*Image does not appear on a Reinthal & Newman postcard, add $25.

Finnish

	VG	EX	NM
Real Photo Type Series	125 - 150	150 - 175	175 - 200

Refer to page 151-153
____All's Well
____Alone at Last
____American Beauties
____Day Dreams
____Drifting
____Fair and Warmer
____June
____My Hero
____A Novice

French

	VG	EX	NM
Affiches De La Grande Guerre	450 - 500	500 - 550	550 - 600

Refer to page 154
____No. 11*

*Image does not appear on a Reinthal & Newman postcard.

German

	VG	EX	NM
Alfred Schweizer/MEU Series	200 - 225	225 - 250	250 - 275

Refer to page 155-156
____Beatrice*
____A Critical Moment*
____In the Country*
____Marcia*
____On the Avenue*
____Rosamond*
____Santa Claus' First Visit*

*Image does not appear on a Reinthal & Newman postcard.

	VG	EX	NM

Polish
Polish & Ukrainian Back Series   125 - 150   150 - 175   175 - 200
Refer to page 157
____A Sprig of Holly
____A Winter Sport
____Winter Whispers

Russian
E.K. Series   150 - 175   175 - 200   200 - 225
Refer to page 158
____No 3   Sweethearts Asleep
____No 4   The Kiss
____No 19   Maid at Arms
____No 25   Dreaming of You

Russian
O.K. & Co. P.   225 - 250   250 - 275   275 - 300
Refer to page 159
____No. 2057 Their Honeymoon Trip (variation)*
*Image does not appear on a Reinthal & Newman postcard.

Russian
English Back Series   175 - 200   200 - 225   225 - 250
Refer to page 160-164
Note: The Series was printed twice with the following issue numbers:
No. 66391 (5,000 pieces)
No. 71293 (3,000 pieces)
____No. 2   To Walk
____No. 3   Dolly*
____No. 7   Friends
____No. 9   Bubbles
____No. 10   June
____No. 12   A Dane
____No. 14   Preparing to Conquer
____No. 15   To Ball
____No. 17   A Rose
____No. 19   Good Night!
____No. 20   Princess Pat
____No. 21   Homeward Bound
____No. 22   Ready and Waiting
____No. 23   To Walk (duplicate title)
____No. 24   Sport
____No. 25   A Prairie Belle
*Image does not appear on a Reinthal & Newman postcard, add $25.

	VG	EX	NM

Russian
Rishar 100 & 800 Series   150 - 175   175 - 200   200 - 225
Refer to page 165-168
____No. 117 Those Bewitching Eyes
____No. 824 Made to Worship
____No. 825 In the Toils
____No. 826 Leisure Moments
____No. 827 The American Beauty*
____No. 828 Teacup Time*
____No. 829 And Yet Her Eyes Can Look Wise
____No. 830 A Taste of Paradise*
____No. 831 Springtime*
____No. 832 Food for Thought*
____No. 833 Lips for Kisses
____No. 834 Vanity
____No. 835 Cherry Ripe
____No. 836 Bewitching Maiden
____No. 837 Polarbear*

*Image does not appear on a Reinthal & Newman postcard, add $25.

Russian
Linen Series   150 - 175   175 - 200   200 - 225
Refer to page 169-171
This series was printed four times with the following issue numbers:
No. 52836 (10,000 pieces)
No. 5350 (15,000 pieces)
No. 5351 (20,000 pieces)
No. 9402 (20,000 pieces)
____No. 1 And Yet Her Eyes Can Look Wise
____No. 2 Leisure Moments
____No. 5 Springtime*
____No. 6 Those Bewitching Eyes
____No. 54 Vanity
____No. 60 Cherry Ripe
____No. 71 Bewitching Maiden
____No. 72 Lips for Kisses

*Image does not appear on a Reinthal & Newman postcard, add $25.

Russian
Sepia Series   150 - 175   175 - 200   200 - 225
Refer to page 172-174
____Bows Attract Beaus
____Courting Attention
____Fine Feathers
____From Life*
____Homeward Bound

	VG	EX	NM
Sepia Series (continued)	150 - 175	175 - 200	200 - 225

    ____Isn't He Sweet?
    ____The Kiss
    ____Maid at Arms
    ____Mary
    ____My Lady Drives
    ____My Pretty Neighbor
    ____Princess Pat
    ____Well Protected

*Image does not appear on a Reinthal & Newman postcard, add $25.

Russian
Real Photo Type Series   175 - 200   200 - 225   225 - 250
Refer to page 175
    ____No. 3221 Maid at Arms
    ____No. 3223 Princess Pat

Russian
AWE Real Photo Type Series   175 - 200   200 - 225   225 - 250
Refer to page 176-177
    ____Beauties
    ____Homeward Bound
    ____Luxury
    ____Miss Knickerbocker
    ____Miss Santa Claus
    ____Roses
    ____Vanity
    ____Well Protected

Russian
Black & White Series   125 - 150   150 - 175   175 - 200
Refer to page 178
    ____Leisure Moments

Russian
Modern Art Sofia Series   75 - 100   100 - 125   125 - 150
Refer to page 179
    ____M.J. S 024 A Kiss
    ____No. 024 A Kiss

Russian
No Identification Series   125 - 150   150 - 175   175 - 200
Refer to page 180
    ____Princess Pat
    ____Sweetheart

	VG	EX	NM

Miscellaneous European (Not Shown)
Marque Depose, Vienne Series 806

____Beatrice*	100 - 125	125 - 150	150 - 175

JTK/Kron-Trier

____A Portrait Sketch*	100 - 125	125 - 150	150 - 175

Friedrich O. Wolter

____Peggy	75 - 100	100 - 125	125 - 150

Chromov & Bachrach

____Miss Santa Claus	250 - 275	275 - 300	300 - 325
____The Rose	125 - 150	150 - 175	175 - 200

*Image does not appear on a Reinthal & Newman Postcard.

Overprints
European Postcards
Refer to page 182

____Autumn's Beauty	250 - 275	275 - 300	300 - 350
Finnish, No Identification Series			
____The Only Pebble	250 - 275	275 - 300	300 - 350
Finnish, No Identification Series			
____The Snow Bird	275 - 300	300 - 325	325 - 350
Finnish, No 30/25 Series			
____A Sprig of Holly	225 - 250	250 - 275	275 - 300
Finnish, Publisher at Polyphot Series			
____Stringing Them	225 - 250	250 - 275	275 - 300
Finnish, No 30/25 Series			
____Welcome Home!	250 - 275	275 - 300	300 - 325
Finnish, No 30/25 Series			
____Winifred	200 - 225	225 - 250	250 - 275
Finnish No 30/25 Series			

____Others*

*Add $50 to the market value of the postcard.